# Sunset

# VISUAL GARDEN MANUAL

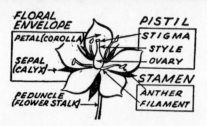

**1.** The function of the flower is to reproduce the plant. For this purpose it contains the organs necessary for reproduction. A "complete" flower contains sepals, petals, stamens and a pistil. A "perfect" flower contains stamens and a pistil, the two essential organs.

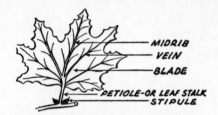

**4.** Leaves, among other things, manufacture starch, digest food, breathe, give off waste and surplus water. The blade contains the working parts of the leaf, the petiole holds the blade to the light, and the veins carry liquids and strengthen the blade.

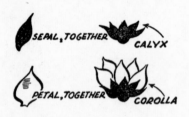

**2.** Sepals are small, leaflike and usually green. Together they form the calyx, a protective sheath which covers the flower while still in bud. Petals are usually colored, leaflike, form a ring inside the sepals, and serve to attract insects.

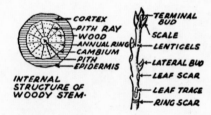

**5.** Stems serve as passageways from leaves to stem and roots, hold leaves up to the sun, manufacture protein, breathe through lenticels, store food (sugar cane, potato), aid climbing (grape), reproduce plants (potato, sugar cane), protect by thorns (crabapple), manufacture food (cactus).

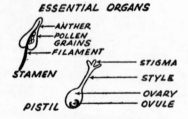

**3.** Stamens are male organs which furnish the pollen for reproduction. The stigma is the female organ. Its sticky top catches the pollen and starts it growing. The style supports the stigma. The ovary forms the fruit, while the ovule becomes a seed.

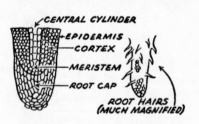

**6.** Roots anchor plants to the ground, absorb moisture and minerals from soil, convert atmospheric nitrogen into nitrates (pea family), store food (carrot), reproduce plants (dahlia), secure food for the plant (mistletoe), aid climbing (ivy), breathe.

THE STRUCTURE OF A PLANT

# Sunset

# VISUAL GARDEN MANUAL

*by*

## ELSA UPPMAN

•

*Illustrated by*
### FRED BARKER
### PHYLLIS GREGG

•

**LANE PUBLISHING CO.** • **SAN FRANCISCO**

TENTH PRINTING, AUGUST, 1949

# PREFACE

It is the hope of those who bring this book to you that it will help to make and to keep gardening simple, enjoyable and understandable. We have thought of the average man or woman who works in the garden after office hours, on weekends, or between washing the breakfast dishes and making lunch. We have thought of busy people to whom gardening is a serious avocation, who want brief, to-the-point answers to their questions.

There will be questions it does not and cannot answer, for it would be impossible to say in one small book all there is to say about gardening in its many phases. There are those gardeners who have explored and studied subjects that have not here been discussed. These we refer to the many publications in specialized fields of horticulture.

A word about *how to use* the following pages. They are divided into "Garden Techniques"—the ABC's of garden operations; "Annuals"; "Perennials"; "Bulbs"; "Shrubs and Trees"; "Special Plants," and "Special Gardens." Each part is arranged alphabetically.

To avoid repetition, elementary steps such as seed sowing are not always shown under each plant's name. These steps will be found under "Garden Techniques." Whenever the general methods shown under the "Techniques" should be varied in the case of an individual plant, we have tried to show that special handling on the page devoted to that plant.

The usefulness of the book can be multiplied many times by reference to the cross-index at the back.

This is a book to be used, and used often. We should like to think of its lying within easy reach on a shelf in the potting-shed or workshop, well-thumbed and perhaps soiled. All who have cooperated to make this book —artists, author, and publisher—want you to make it a handbook and a guide to a wider, fuller, and more interesting experience in your garden. Special mention is due James Kerr, Frank Cuthbertson, Clarence Hoff and Norvell Gillespie for their suggestions.

Fundamentally, gardening is simple. Its beginnings were simple and elemental. Men began to work in the soil long before the days of recorded history. The need and the urge to grow plants for use or pleasure are so ingrained in man that he will find, even under the most adverse conditions, a way to satisfy them.

Succeeding generations have added new chapters to its story. With the development of science and the introduction of new plants, new tools,

(CONTINUED ON NEXT PAGE)

# PREFACE (continued)

new fertilizers and new methods, gardening has outwardly taken on a more complex and varied nature, but the principles remain the same.

Gardeners are not magicians and a real gardener never pretends to be one. He knows that, in order to succeed, he must work in close collaboration with certain fundamental laws of nature. And so he does not attempt to grow tropical plants where temperatures fall to zero, nor alpines in the desert. Careful observation means as much in gardening as in any activity.

Most gardeners are a patient lot. They will spend months, even years, trying to grow a difficult or capricious plant, only to lose it in a frost, a drought, through gophers, some pest or disease. Undaunted, they will end up by growing another quite as difficult. Such is their answer to the challenge of adversity!

Real gardeners are rarely, if ever, bored. Seasonal changes and variations, the study of soils, the introduction of new and rare plants: these are a few of the things that make gardening one of the most interesting and stimulating of professions and pastimes, one in which the interchange of ideas is endless.

A real gardener is rarely discouraged or depressed. How can one, for instance, dread the approach of winter or believe in the cessation of growth when at the time that snow blankets the ground and ice covers the pond one sees buds swelling and the first tender tips of the snowdrop and crocus breaking through the ground? And what gardener does not sit by the fire on a rainy or snowy night with seed catalogues about him, making longer and longer lists, ordering packet after packet of seeds, and dreaming dreams of summer gardens? Time for boredom? Hurry—seeds sown in February bloom in May and June!

It is said that the best things in life are free. Whether this be strictly true or not, the best things in life can and should be shared. Sharing them, we learn from one another. This might be called the gardeners' creed. It is the basis of this book.

Yes, the soil gives us more than flowers that are beautiful to look at or fruits and vegetables that are good to eat. It gives us hope, courage, patience and quiet joy. It anchors us to something solid, fundamental, timeless and constructive. It binds us to the best in man's heritage, a heritage rooted in a desire which could find its first expression only after men had ceased preying upon one another and will find its highest when men again settle down to live and work in peace.

*Elsa Uppman*

# CONTENTS

## GARDEN TECHNIQUES

## ANNUALS

## PERENNIALS

# CONTENTS (continued)

# GARDEN TECHNIQUES

Here are the *ways* to do things, the fundamentals which form the foundation of your garden. You will want to use it often, for your garden is as good as the soil of which it is composed and the methods used to maintain and improve it. Your way of planting, feeding, watering, pruning, etc., will determine the appearance and longevity of your plants. When reading other parts of this book (about this or that given plant), you will find it constantly worthwhile to refer back to "Garden Techniques."

# BUDDING

SELECT GOOD STOCK AND BUDS

**1.** Plants to be budded must, as a rule, be closely related. The plant growing in the ground is called the *stock*. The *bud* is cut from another plant and inserted in the stock. Select strong, vigorous buds and stocks with the qualities you wish to see perpetuated.

INSERTED BUD

**4.** Working quickly and handling the bud as little as possible, insert the bud in the lower end of the inverted T. Light pressure may be required to slip the bud into place, but care must be taken not to tear the bark around the T.

CUT UNDER BARK — THE BUD

**2.** The shield-bud is cut from a young twig of the present season's (spring) growth. Cut with a sharp, clean knife under the bark to the cambium layer beneath. Work quickly and do not let the bud dry out. Commercial growers water subjects to be budded a few days prior to the operation. This makes the bark slip and peel more easily.

TIED

**5.** The cambium layers of the stock and bud fit closely together. Now tie the bud and wound securely with raffia or a stout rubber band. This method of tieing makes constriction of the bud impossible.

T-SHAPED CUT IN BARK

**3.** Make a clean T-shaped cut (with the T upside down) in the bark of the stock. Gently pry back the bark to facilitate insertion of the bud. You will see the exposed cambium layer of the stock.

CUT STOCK HERE AS SCION GROWS — THE NEXT SPRING

**6.** With growth of the bud the raffia or rubber band will be stretched until it breaks or rots away. As the bud grows, cut back the stock slightly. The following spring the old stub of the stock can be entirely cut off.

# BULBS

FLESHY SCALES

TRUE BULBS    CORM

RHIZOME    TUBER

**1.** *Bulbs* are *scaly* (lily) or *laminate* (onion). A *corm* is solid and bulb-like (gladiolus). A *rhizome* or *rootstock* is a swollen stem of a perennial plant (iris). A *tuber* is a thickened portion of a root or stem (dahlia).

INCORRECT    CORRECT

AIR POCKET WHERE ROT MAY START—    SAND

**4.** To avoid losing bulbs through improper drainage, prepare bulb beds in the following way: Dig deeply (18"-20") and bury well-rotted manure (never allow bulbs to contact fresh manure); place bulbs on a cushion of sand, and fill in with rich loose soil.

**2.** While different bulbs require different planting conditions, most of them prefer sunny locations. Exceptions include true lilies, lilies-of-the-valley and begonias. Bulbs have a wide range of uses, as: cut flowers, pot plants, in special bulb gardens or beds, in mixed borders and in some cases, rock gardens.

**5.** Usually one soaking will be sufficient for a bulb planting until leaves begin to appear, especially for spring-flowering bulbs, such as daffodils, crocus, etc. Summer-flowering bulbs such as gladiolus and dahlias need regular waterings throughout their active growing season.

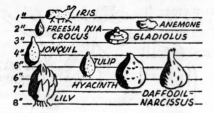

1"  IRIS
2"  FREESIA IXIA    ANEMONE
     CROCUS    GLADIOLUS
4"  JONQUIL
6"  TULIP
6"
7"  HYACINTH
     LILY    DAFFODIL
8"    NARCISSUS

**3.** Many bulbs can be planted twice their own depth. Exceptions are iris, which should be planted with the rhizome above the surface of the soil. Plant daffodils and other narcissi deeply enough to allow planting and cultivation of other plants above and between them.

**6.** When flowers are faded and bulb foliag. has yellowed and withered, one may cut of the tops, but never before! When cutting of tops, leave 2"-3" for protection of the bulb. Completely dry foliage may be pulled off.

# COLDFRAME

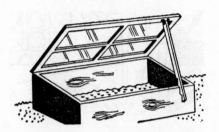

**1.** The coldframe gives winter protection to tender plants and pushes lagging plants in spring. The single-sash type is a convenient one where only a corner can be spared. Construct it of redwood and creosote the bottom as a protection against termites.

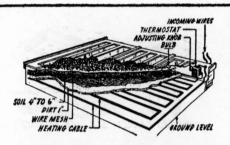

**4.** The electrically-heated hotbed, with its waterproofed, lead-insulated cable, is the most dependable method of heating frames. The thermostatic control maintains a uniform temperature. Cuttings, seedlings and potted plants will grow twice as rapidly in this hotbed.

**2.** This two-purpose frame is divided in the center. In the glass-covered section can be grown half-hardy plants and cuttings, in the lath-covered side hardy plants and pricked-out seedlings when they are large enough to leave shelter and get ready for life outside.

**5.** Frames are versatile. One can grow plants directly in the soil, or in pots or flats which can be placed on the bottom. Or the pots can be sunk up to their rims in peat, sand, wood shavings, or gravel. The latter method is excellent during the warmer months when pots are apt to dry out rapidly.

**3.** A mixture of ⅔ horse manure and ⅓ leaves makes a good heating medium for hotbeds. Stack them, keep them wet and turned for about a week. In 10 or 11 days they will be ready for the hotbed. Place 18″ of manure in bottom, pack it well, add 5″-6″ of soil on top. Grow plants directly in the soil or in pots.

**6.** Frames can carry over young plants until they are ready to be set out. For instance, geranium cuttings after being potted up can be plunged in their pots in frames, to remain for 2 months, or until sturdy enough to plant out.

# COMPOSTING

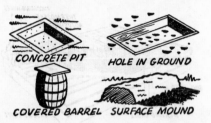

**1.** The *concrete pit* holds moisture, keeps out pests, and is easy to keep clean. Line the *hole in the ground* with redwood treated with creosote. The *covered barrel* is ideal for the small garden. A large amount of compost should be piled in a long, *narrow mound*.

**4.** The compost heap should be turned and stirred with a pitchfork every 2 or 3 weeks to aid the decomposing, mellowing process. Leave it stacked compactly, water it thoroughly after mixing to aid fermentation and decomposition.

**2.** The refuse you would ordinarily burn or send off with the garbage goes into the compost heap. Humus, composed of decayed or decaying vegetable matter, is the best base for organic fertilizers. It contains food and improves the mechanical condition of the soil.

**5.** 3 to 6 months are required to make a compost. A good compost is rich and dark in color, light and friable in texture, sweet-smelling, and soft and moist to touch. Substitute it for leafmold in potting and seed-sowing mixtures.

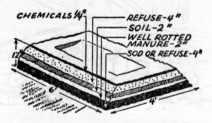

**3.** By storing materials in layers, as in the diagram, rapid decomposition and a rich compost will result. The scattering of lime, gypsum or a commercial preparation specifically intended for composts keeps away unpleasant odors. Add sand for a heavy, clayey soil.

**6.** Nothing can equal compost as a base for commercial fertilizers. Use it as a top dressing for lawns, on flower beds and around trees and shrubs. When making over old flower beds, spade it in generously; use it as a mulch after the bed is planted.

# CULTIVATION

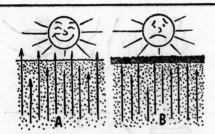

**1.** Through multitudes of tiny tubes between soil particles moisture escapes from the sub-soil to the surface and out into the atmosphere. To stop this escape it is necessary to break these capillary tubes by cultivating or by spreading a layer of fine, loose material, such as peat, over the surface.

**4.** Weeds are greedy. They rob flowers of valuable food, water and growing space. Unusually vigorous, they outgrow their aristocratic neighbors; unless uprooted or cut down, they will soon crowd them out. Weeds are unsightly, too, and an indication of a poorly kept garden

**2.** Uncultivated, unmulched plants suffer from malnutrition, because certain bacteria responsible for the release of necessary food elements cannot work in dry, uncultivated soil Cultivating helps to prevent shallow-rootedness and wilting, and aerates the soil.

**5.** Peat moss, compost (see Index on Composts), mushroom fertilizer, and grass clippings can be used as mulches. For best results, water thoroughly, cultivate 2 or 3 days later, and spread mulching material at least 2" deep. It should not be necessary to water again until 10 or 12 days have passed.

**3.** The *four-pronged cultivator* leaves soil fine-textured; the diamond-shaped *push-hoe* cultivates, weeds, digs and edges; the V-shaped *Warren hoe* is used for cultivating and making furrows; the *hand-weeder* is good for use among small plants; the *cultivator-hoe* works two ways, as does the familiar *garden hoe*.

**6.** Mulching benefits all trees and shrubs. Some, such as rhododendrons, azaleas and camellias, demand a summer mulch. A 3" or 4" mulch of peat moss, pine or redwood needles or rotted oak leaves is the safest and best method for keeping them in good condition.

# CUTTING FLOWERS

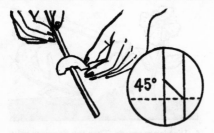

**1.** Breaking flowers from their stalks, picking them in the heat of the day and allowing them to remain out of water, are unpardonable sins. Cut with shears or a sharp knife (see illustration for a knife giving a 45° cut). Cut them in the early morning or evening.

**4.** Make a new cut every morning, empty the old water and refill the container with fresh water. Many flowers daily drink an incredible amount of water; a new cut starts anew the flow of moisture up the stem.

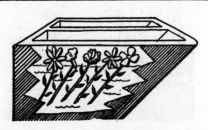

**2.** Plunge flowers immediately in deep cold water in laundry tubs or deep buckets. Heavy-headed, weak-necked flowers, such as tulips, will straighten and stiffen up amazingly if placed firmly and evenly in bunches, rolled tightly in newspaper, and plunged up to their necks in water over night.

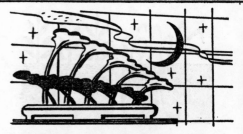

**5.** Flowers and leaves breathe. Close house atmospheres exhaust most of their surface moisture. Place them on a screened porch or in a window where they can breathe deeply of cool, moist air. Limp stems and leaves will stiffen and worn flowers revive.

**3.** Some flowers, such as dahlias, oriental poppies, poinsettias and heliotrope keep better if their cut stems are put into hot water (about 170°) for a few seconds, after which they should be placed in deep containers of cool water.

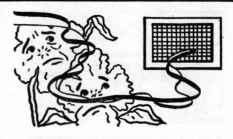

**6.** Give your cut flowers a "break"! Don't place them near radiators, heaters, fireplaces or in direct sunlight. Strong drafts of air are also to be avoided.

# CUTTINGS

**1.** Soft-wooded cuttings are usually made from sideshoots of plants. They are ready to be taken when they snap off cleanly. Shoots that bend or crush are too young or too old. Stem cuttings can be softwooded (geranium) or hardwooded (privet).

**4.** Many soft-wooded cuttings root in 4-8 weeks, though some take longer. When a cutting has several strong roots, pot it up in a 3" or 4" pot, using a seed-sowing mixture. Shade newly potted cuttings for a few days. Keep moist, but not wet.

**2.** Using a sharp knife, make a clean, slanting cut about ¼" below a node (or leaf axil). Remove all but 2 or 3 leaves at the top. If these leaves are large, trim them back ⅓ to ⅔ to reduce evaporation.

**5.** After 7-8 weeks, the roots of the cutting will be showing through the hole in the bottom of the pot. It will then be ready to pot on (see Potting) or plant in its permanent place in the open ground.

**3.** Dip the newly made cuttings in hormone powder (see Hormones), and firmly insert them in sand. A deep box with a 3" layer of No. 2 sand is best. A glass or cello-glass top will afford the close atmosphere necessary for most cuttings.

**6.** Prepare the ground carefully before planting. Tip the plant out of the pot without disturbing the roots and plant in a cushion of peat. In warm weather, shade with laths or paper; in cold weather, protect with paper protectors. Water every other day until established.

# DISBUDDING AND PINCHING BACK

**1.** Pinching-back helps to make weak, spindly plants strong and bushy. It stimulates new growth and equalizes or balances top and root growth. Most plants, especially annuals, such as stock, snapdragons, marigolds, etc., should be pinched back when they are 6"-10" high.

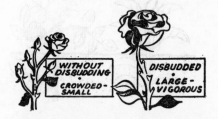

**4.** A plant that is not disbudded will frequently "bloom itself out" due to over-production of flowers and seeds. Out of 6 buds at the top of a stem, only 2 or 3 should be left—or, if an exhibition flower is desired, only one.

**2.** Not only will a plant be bushier and stronger after being pinched back, but it will produce more flowers. Energy wasted in making unwanted leaves and stems will go into flowers instead. There will also be a longer season of bloom.

**5.** The careful gardener picks off affected parts of plants before the attack has a chance to spread. When leaf curl appears on peaches, mildew or rust on roses, or wilt on asters or tomatoes, pick the affected leaves and quickly burn them.

**3.** Disbudding is especially necessary on such plants as roses, dahlias, and chrysanthemums, which produce many buds at the top of the stem. Pinch out side buds while they are still small and easy to nip or pick off. Carefully remove the bud and its stem to the main stem.

**6.** Cutting faded blooms is a form of pruning. Here are the results: A longer period of bloom, larger flowers (due to the fact that less energy will be spent in seed-production), and a more attractive-looking plant. Not a bad bargain for so little trouble!

# DIVIDING

**1.** All but tap-rooted perennials can be propagated by division, the easiest and most usual method of increasing stock. Some can be divided or separated very easily, since they naturally come apart in certain divisions; others must be forced with the help of a knife, fork or spade.

**4.** While most perennials have ordinary root systems, the rhizome, or rootstock (ex. iris) is a swollen underground stem; fibrous roots (ex. fibrous-rooted begonia) may be divided into pieces consisting of root and shoot; runners are prostrate shoots that root at the joints. (ex. strawberry).

**2.** It is a wise practice to go through one's garden periodically to check on times and quality of bloom and to tag plants while still flowering. This eliminates confusion at dividing and replanting time and assures use of only satisfactory material and colors.

**5.** Frequently perennials, such as Michaelmas daisies or helianthus, make such tight, thickly rooted clumps that it is impossible to divide them by the usual methods. The following method is recommended: Insert two forks back to back in the center of the clump, pry the handles apart. Even the toughest will yield.

**3.** Most perennials need dividing every 3 years. Iris roots intertwine and overcrowd after 2 or 3 years, and the clump rises higher and higher above-ground. It should be lifted, separated into single-rooted divisions and replanted. Plant in a sunny, well-drained position with top of rhizome exposed to the sun.

**6.** Separate perennials into fairly small divisions, since they increase rapidly and soon become crowded. A general rule is to plant divisions 12″-18″ apart, depending on the ultimate size of the plant. Small campanulas, etc., can be planted 12″ apart; Michaelmas daisies, etc., 18″ to 2′ apart.

# DRAINAGE

**1.** When trees are planted on top of hardpan their roots are forced sideways. Such hardpan should be broken up with a pick-axe, the poor soil removed, and the bottom of the hole filled with drainage. Then place a thick layer of topsoil, and plant the tree.

**4.** Trenching, or double-digging improves drainage. Mark space to be trenched into 2′ sections, except for the first, which is 2½′. Remove topsoil to a spade's depth from the first section; place it at the end of the border. Fork manure into the first ditch, then fill with topsoil from the second ditch. In the last ditch put topsoil from the first.

**2.** The ditch for a single tile drain should be 2′ to 3′ deep and slant 3″ to every 100′. Fill the bottom with 6″ of coarse gravel, place 4″ concrete tiles end to end. Cover the joints with tar paper to ensure against clogging by loose soil. Cover with 6″ of gravel, and fill the ditch with topsoil.

**5.** A perfectly drained seedbed is essential for many plants, such as alpines. At the bottom, place a wire screen to keep out rodents, next a 3″ layer of gravel, then 6″ of sifted compost, and lastly a 1″ top layer of cinders.

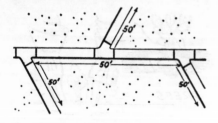

**3.** The herringbone pattern is used for large areas (an acre or more) and tiles are laid as in the single ditch. Lateral ditches are run off at a slant every 50′. As in the single ditch, the entire system should gradually drop toward the point to which the water is being carried.

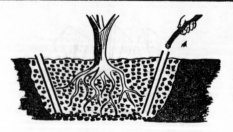

**6.** A boxed tree demands and deserves this special treatment. Work gypsum into the subsoil to break up heavy clay and make it more friable. The 1″ pipes at either side of the ball carry water and food directly to the roots. Plenty of good soil on all sides of the ball encourages new roots.

# ESPALIERING

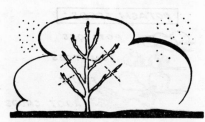

**1.** To espalier a fruit tree, plant a 1-year-old whip on bare root in winter. Prune back to 18"-24". Later, when sideshoots grow, decide on the type of espalier and select the branches required. Dwarf stock is best for espaliers. Regularly sized trees are apt to become too large to train properly.

**2.** For a horizontal cordon, select and tie two laterals in a horizontal position. The *espalier* differs from this form only in the fact that a center stem is also retained, pruned to about 18" and firmly tied in an upright position.

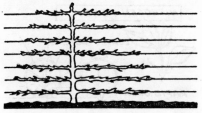

**3.** The following year, cut back the center shoot to 18" and again select and tie two side-branches. Continue selecting and training in successive years until there are 5 or more tiers, and the espalier is about 10' high. Pinch back shoots in summer to encourage fruiting and to produce good form.

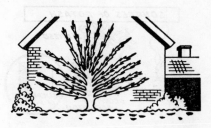

**4.** The fan-shaped espalier is especially adapted to small stone fruits and to growing against walls (east or north exposure). Retain stems of equal strength the first year. Next year cut back the center shoot hard, thus encouraging new shoots from one point.

**5.** The gridiron is also suitable for growing against walls. Train as for the espalier, except that when branches have grown horizontally 7' or 8', they are trained upwards, usually to about 10'. Apples and pears are well adapted to this form.

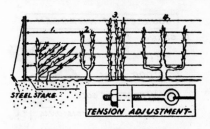

**6.** For an *oblique cordon*, cut back all but one strong stem. Tie this at an angle. The *upright cordon* is a one-stemmed tree with all laterals pruned back hard. The *triple cordon* is like the gridiron with the center and two outside branches removed.

# FERTILIZERS

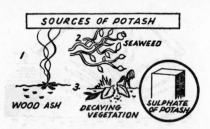

### SOURCES OF POTASH

SEAWEED

WOOD ASH

DECAYING VEGETATION

SULPHATE OF POTASH

**1.** A high percentage of potash is present in woodash, especially in ashes of young prunings, in seaweed, burned or unburned, and in the leaves of crops such as beets and potatoes. More concentrated forms of potash are found in mineral compounds.

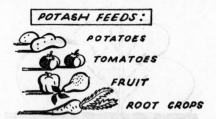

### POTASH FEEDS:

POTATOES

TOMATOES

FRUIT

ROOT CROPS

**4.** Potash is very important for the development of many food crops high in carbohydrate value, for the development of fruit, for seed production, and for resistance of plants to pests and diseases. Root crops, such as beets, carrots, turnips and radishes especially require potash.

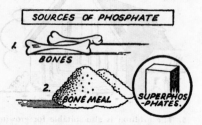

### SOURCES OF PHOSPHATE

1. BONES

2. BONE MEAL

SUPERPHOS-PHATES.

**2.** Bones and guanos are high in phosphates. One of the best and safest forms is steamed bonemeal, a fertilizer which is good for almost all but acid-loving plants. Superphosphates, usually containing mineral phosphates or guano and bones, are rich fertilizers.

### PHOSPHATE FEEDS:

ROOT GROWTH

FRUIT & FLOWERS

FOOD CROPS

**5.** Phosphates promote root growth. Cereals, vegetables and flowers need them, as do crops connected with dairying. The larger root area which results from phosphatic fertilizers enables plants to root deeply, and to resist drought, pests and diseases.

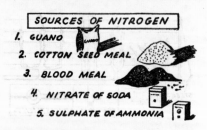

### SOURCES OF NITROGEN

1. GUANO

2. COTTON SEED MEAL

3. BLOOD MEAL

4. NITRATE OF SODA

5. SULPHATE OF AMMONIA

**3.** Nitrogen, the most important fertilizing element, is found in many organic and chemical fertilizers. Nitrogenous fertilizers are expensive, quickly used and therefore need frequent replacement. Nitrate of soda and sulphate of ammonia are the two most important nitrogenous chemical fertilizers.

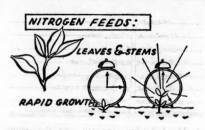

### NITROGEN FEEDS:

LEAVES & STEMS

RAPID GROWTH

**6.** Nitrogen stimulates leaf and stem growth. It is particularly important for leaf crops, such as spinach and lettuce. It is quick acting, and revives jaded crops after a cold spell or an attack of pests or disease. Nitrogenous fertilizers must be used with great care.

# FERTILIZING

### ANNUALS OR PERENNIALS

RING FERTILIZER—
WATER AFTERWARD

**1.** Commercial fertilizers are concentrated. Use them moderately and regularly, not heavily and spasmodically. A teaspoon to a plant is usually enough. Work the fertilizer into the soil and water immediately afterwards.

### TREES

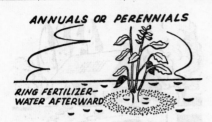

←2″→
FERTILIZER
SET IN HOLES
AROUND
TREE

**4.** The feeding roots of trees are at the tips of large roots. They can best be reached by making holes in a ring in line with the outside spread of the tree. Make 4 times as many holes as there are pounds of fertilizer to be used. A tree with a 10′ spread will take 2½ pounds of fertilizer and 10 holes.

### BULBS

SOIL
BULB
SAND

RING OF
FERTILIZER

BONE MEAL
AT BOTTOM
BEFORE PLANTING

**2.** Bonemeal is the ideal fertilizer for most bulbs. It is safe, long-lasting in effect, and easy to use. Second and third-year bulbs will give gratifying results if planted with one tablespoonful of bonemeal in each hole. Mix it well with the soil.

### LAWNS

**5.** Feed ordinary lawns with a complete fertilizer every fall and spring. Bent lawns need a monthly feeding through the growing season, usually one with a high nitrogen content. Topdress lawns yearly with a compost containing commercial fertilizer. Some advise spiking lawns and sweeping in ¼″ of sand to aerate and improve drainage.

### ROSES AND SHRUBS

**3.** Most flowering shrubs are heavy feeders. Roses are especially so and should be fed at regular 2- or 3-week intervals during the growing season. Scatter fertilizer in a basin around each plant, work in with a trowel or hand-fork, and water.

### HOUSE PLANTS

**6.** Feed potted plants from the time of the first appearance of the buds until they begin to show color. Liquid manure or 1 teaspoon of commercial fertilizer to a pot is considered safe and sufficient. Never feed a dry or sickly plant.

# FROST CONTROL

**1.** Frost affects plants in much the same way as heat or drought. The best way to avoid loss from frost is to use as much as possible hardy plant material. Occasionally, however, even the most cautious gardener is fooled. How can plants be protected?

**4.** The best protection against loss of heat by convection is a system of barriers, in the form of hedges, fences, walls, shrubbery masses and windbreaks. Drying-off plants increases concentration of the cell sap and so makes them better able to withstand cold.

**2.** One way in which heat leaves the ground is through *radiation*, or heat waves, especially on clear nights. To stop radiation, use burlap coverings, laths, pergolas and arbors over tender plants. Branching trees and shrubs and heavy vines also help.

**5.** Cold air, being heavy, moves downward, while warm air goes upward. Hillside gardens should be planted with this fact in view. Hardy, late-flowering or late-bearing plants should be planted at the bottom of the slope, the less hardy at the top.

**3.** The direct contact of cold air with a warm surface is called *convection* or *conduction*. The colder the air the more rapidly it travels; the more rapid its movement the colder it becomes. An open, unprotected garden is easy prey to killing frosts.

**6.** Frosted plants reached by early morning sunshine are more apt to be lost than those not touched until later. To effect a gradual thawing-out, sprinkle frosted plants with water before the sun reaches them. Also, place tender plants out of range of early winter sun.

# GRAFTING

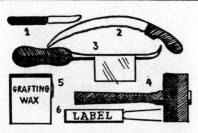

**1.** Grafting is the process of bringing together the growing regions of two plants to make them unite and grow as one. Tools necessary are (1) knife for cleaning the cut, (2) a curved saw for cutting branches, (3) a knife for making the cleft, (4) a mallet, (5) grafting wax to seal the cut, (6) labels.

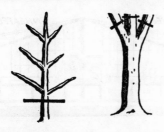

**2.** The best time for cleft grafting is just before growth starts, usually in late winter or early spring. Branches or trees 1½"-2" in diameter are most satisfactory, though branches 4" or more in diameter can also be grafted. Very large trees should be worked during more than one season.

**3.** In making the cleft, or split in the branch or trunk, see that no knot is in line with the cut. Make the cleft directly in the middle of the trunk or limb. A mallet will be necessary to drive in the knife.

**4.** The branch or trunk to be grafted is called the stock. The part inserted in the stock is the scion or cion. The scion, cut from a twig or shoot of the past season's growth, should have 2 or 3 buds, usually 3, and is given its wedge-shaped end with two strokes of a sharp knife.

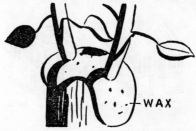

**5.** Insert the wedge of the scion into the cleft of the stock. Take care to see that the growing, or cambium layers of the scion and stock, are closely matched, or union will not take place. Next cover the cut surfaces with grafting wax.

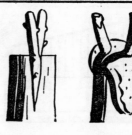

**6.** If the graft is successful, buds will swell and leaves appear on the scions. However, not until 3 or 4 months later can one be certain that the union is completely made. One year later the two parts will have become as one.

# GREENHOUSES

**1.** Prefabricated, knockdown models and simple construction have brought the greenhouse within reach of almost every home gardener. With a little help, a man who is handy with tools can put up a 3-section greenhouse in one or two days. This model measures about 7½' x 11½'.

**4.** Here is a modern version of the conservatory, which was part of many an old mansion in the late 1800's and early 1900's. Decorative, useful, space saving, it is admirably suited to town gardens. It can be heated by the same system as that serving the house.

**2.** If possible, place greenhouses on level ground, with the ridgepole running north to south, so as to get the maximum amount of sunshine. The foundation can be of concrete, brick or of creosoted redwood planks. In 4 sections, this measures 11' x 15'.

**5.** A large greenhouse requires much heat. In climates where cold is not too extreme for most plants, the building can be divided. One side, heated, can be used for propagating and for tender plants. The other side, unheated, houses hardy plants.

**3.** The lean-to is the simplest greenhouse. Against the wall of a house, shed or garage, it should harmonize with the architecture of the main building. It is well adapted to the growing of shade plants, on a north or east wall. In hot exposures, heavy shading is necessary, except for cacti and heat-loving plants.

**6.** A sunny window or alcove can resemble a small glorified greenhouse. Glass shelves will not obstruct light. Unless the window faces north or east, only sun-loving, flowering plants or cacti and succulents should be grown.

# GREENHOUSE CULTURE

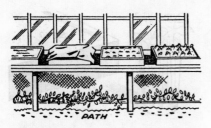

**1.** Originally, greenhouses were structures in which plants were kept alive or green through the winter. Their chief use now is for starting plants early in the season. Seeds can be sown and plants will bloom 4 to 6 weeks earlier if started indoors.

**4.** The amateur can grow orchids if he has a heated greenhouse and observes the following rules: Keep the temperature between 50° and 60°; the atmosphere and the moss about the orchid roots must be moist; over-watering in winter must be avoided; protect from burning sun.

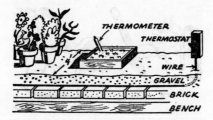

**2.** Most cuttings root more quickly in a greenhouse, especially if the cutting bench is heated by an electric cable, as in the diagram. Satisfactory results can be had by placing cuttings in boxes rather than directly in soil above the cable.

**5.** Tomatoes and cucumbers should be started from seed about 10 weeks before planting time and planted out when they have two sets of leaves. Plant 3½' apart in benches filled with rich soil. Night temperatures should be around 60°, day temperatures about 65°. Pinch to a single stem and tie to wires.

**3.** Potted plants and bulbs can be forced into bloom several weeks early in a greenhouse. Pot up winter-flowering plants and bulbs in September to have them in flower by December or January. Forcing caps will bring up to the light bulbs that are blooming low.

**6.** Many of the potted plants grown for porch, terrace and patio decoration are too tender to be kept outdoors in winter. Protected in the greenhouse, they can be started off in the spring with a light pruning, repotting, and feeding, ready for another season's use.

# HORMONES

**1.** Growth hormones are chemicals manufactured within the plant and used by the plant to develop stems and roots. They have been called "chemical messengers." Some hormones originate in the roots and travel up to the stem; others move from leaves to roots.

**2.** Hormone preparations are synthetically produced and sold in powder and solution forms. Powders are easiest to use. One solution is made by dissolving 1/10 gram Indole Acetic acid crystals in 10 cc. pure grain alcohol. One cc. of solution is used for each 100 cc. of water. Indolebutyric acid is also used.

**3.** Hormone preparations are used to stimulate the formation of root primordia or cuttings. Their usefulness is past once roots are formed. Procedure is as follows: Make cuttings, dip their ends in hormone powder, then insert in sand, as usual.

**4.** If solution is used, make the cuttings in the usual way, then stand them in a glass containing enough solution (or about 1") to cover their ends. Let them stand 22 to 24 hours. Then insert them in coarse sand.

**5.** A deep box is best for cuttings. Provide ¾" holes in the bottom, a layer of drainage and 3"-4" of clean, coarse sand. Pack and moisten the sand before inserting the cuttings. Use a dibber or pointed stick for firming-in.

**6.** Cuttings treated with hormone preparations will frequently respond more rapidly than those not treated. For instance, cuttings ordinarily taking 2 months to root will, when treated with hormone powder or acid solution, take only 4 to 6 weeks.

# HYDROPONICS

**1.** Plants can be grown without soil if the chemicals necessary to plant life are adequately supplied. This method is called Hydroponics or Water Culture and is in many ways simpler than growing plants in soil. Various chemical preparations for soilless culture are offered commercially.

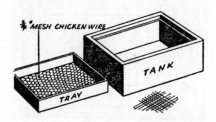

**2.** The tank and tray necessary for water culture can be almost any size desired. A convenient size is 1½' by 2½'. Materials can be redwood or galvanized iron. Both must be painted with asphalt varnish to prevent unfavorable chemical action.

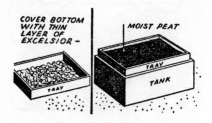

**3.** The tray should be about 4" deep and have a bottom of chicken wire. Over the wire place a layer of excelsior, then fill the tray with moist peat or sphagnum moss. The tray should be made so as to fit inside the tank.

**4.** The tank should be at least 8" deep. If a commercial preparation is used to make the solution, the nutrients are already mixed in correct proportions. If mixing your own chemicals, follow carefully a scientific formula. Aeration and agitation of the solution are important factors in hydroponics.

**5.** Annuals, perennials, bulbs and vegetables can be grown without soil. Such plants as squash and cucumbers are often sown directly in the litter (peat or moss). Plants can be started in soil and later transplanted to the tray. Sand and gravel are proving most successful mediums for water culture.

**6.** From time to time it will be necessary to add more nutrients, or chemicals, to replenish those already used by the growing plants. Excellent results have been reported with tulips, hyacinths, tomatoes, cucumbers, squash and beans.

# LANDSCAPING

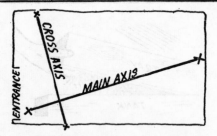

**1.** Even the smallest garden requires planning. First draw in the boundaries, then the main axis, usually a diagonal line extending from the main entrance or point from which the garden is best viewed, to an important feature, perhaps a pool, sundial or bird bath.

**4.** Certain shrubs and trees lend themselves admirably to screening or blocking out. Pines, the finer acacias, casuarinas and tamarix make quick growing backgrounds and screens. California cherry, cytisus, escallonia, genista, leptospermum and rhamnus are good shrubs for this purpose.

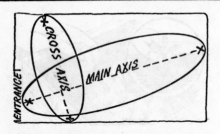

**2.** A minor axis crossing the main axis gives opportunities for additional points of interest, such as fine flowering trees, or unusual shrubs. Draw ovals around these axes. Place lawns inside the ovals, borders and shrubbery outside. The backbone of your garden is now ready.

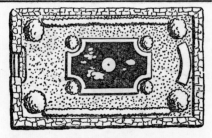

**5.** Formal gardens are easy to design and lay out and are well adapted to small as well as large spaces. Much of their charm lies in clipped hedges and shrubs, trim lawns and well kept paths. This means constant upkeep.

**3.** A certain amount of blocking out is necessary in almost every town or city garden. To block out successfully, it is well to know the ultimate height and spread of trees and shrubs, whether they are fast or slow growing, light or heavy in texture.

**6.** The informal garden is more difficult to design but simpler to maintain. Its lines are for the most part curving. Shrubbery is planted in groups of 3, 5 or 7 plants, lawn edges are gently undulating (not scalloped!) and flower beds can be similarly informal.

# LATHHOUSES

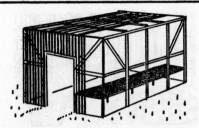

**1.** There is a lathhouse for almost every garden and purse. The rectangular type is one of the simplest to build and can be large or small. An adequate size for the average garden is 9' x 14'. Lathhouses should face north to south, away from large trees. Avoid high roofs, a good height is 8'.

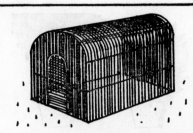

**4.** A curved roof makes the ordinary flat-topped lathhouse more decorative. In cool, foggy districts space the laths farther apart, especially on the top, to admit more sunlight. In hot, dry windy sections space them closer than usual. Glass coverings on the windy side are especially helpful.

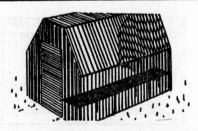

**2.** In even the small town garden there should be space for a lathhouse measuring 8' x 8'. It is inexpensive and easy to build. A good feature is the sloping side which is fastened with hinges, thus enabling one to admit full sunlight when desired. Being portable, it is an ideal lathhouse for the garden-minded renter.

**5.** A glass-covered frame is frequently too warm for many plants. The lath covering over the top of the frame gives shade without cutting out needed light. For cuttings that must be kept "close," keep the window down and put the lath on top.

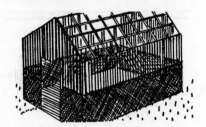

**3.** Here is the "super" lathhouse. Its glass roof makes it a hybrid, a lathhouse-glasshouse, serving a double purpose. For extra cold weather protection, a five-foot strip of burlap can be tacked on the outside. This lathhouse will not do for tender plants where the temperature drops below 24°.

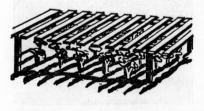

**6.** This simple lath frame stands high enough to clear the tops of young plants and offers ample shade, but does not cut off needed light or circulation. Such protection may decide the success or failure of a planting during a hot spell.

# LATHHOUSE CULTURE

**1.** Lathhouses help to solve the problem of what to do with shade-loving plants before, after and during their blooming season. The laths are far enough apart to admit light and circulation necessary for flowering plants, yet protect from hot sun and drying winds.

**4.** The transfer of young plants from the greenhouse to the lathhouse or the outdoors is called "hardening off." The adjustment to outside conditions is a gradual one and plants will suffer little or no shock when finally planted in their permanent positions.

**2.** Plants that thrive in lathhouses are tuberous and fibrous begonias, ferns, cyclamen, fuchsias, hydrangeas, azaleas and camellias. Enough protection is afforded to encourage heavy flowering, yet the atmosphere and temperature are moist and cool enough to prevent drying out and early fading of blooms.

**5.** The summer care of such shade-loving plants as cinerarias is often difficult. The lathhouse is an ideal location for them during the hot months. It may be necessary to spray them with water twice a day if their leaves appear wilted.

**3.** Gardeners who do not have lathhouses frequently ask where they should keep their flats of plants before setting them out, and their potted plants both before and after blooming. The closest substitute is to be found under shade trees. Keep flats and pots off the ground and protect from dripping leaves.

**6.** Lathhouses can take on the appearance of conservatories or arbors if one hangs baskets or pots of begonias, ferns, fuchsias, campanulas or other trailing plants. Another decorative note results from planting lush green ground covers such as Irish moss or maidenhair fern under the benches.

# LAYERING

**1.** Layering is an easy and convenient method of increasing plants. Many herbaceous plants as well as shrubs can be propagated this way. Among them are dianthus, aubrieta, berberis, peony, daphne, rhododendron and azalea. Prepare beforehand the ground in which layering is to be done.

**4.** With certain hard-wooded shrubs, such as rhododendron and azalea, old branches are layered. They must be buried at least 4″ deep, or to the point of the previous year's growth. Surround the layered portion with a mixture of sand and peat to help along rooting.

**2.** Bend down the branch, make a slit underneath, and insert a pebble to hold it open. This stimulates roots. Hold the layered stem in place with a peg, cover with soil in which some sand and peat have been mixed; support the upright shoot with a stake.

**5.** After completing the layering operation and the staking of the end of the branch, place a brick or stone as a weight over the layer. Not only will this hold the branch firmly in place, but it will help prevent drying out.

**3.** Layers of soft-wooded plants, such as dianthus, often root in 6-8 weeks. When they are rooted, sever with a sharp knife from the parent plant. Pot up or plant out in well prepared soil. Keep buds pinched off until a good root system is developed.

**6.** Most layers are rooted within 1 year. Often the layered plant is severed from the mother plant and allowed to remain in the ground until its root system is well established. Rhododendron layers usually take 2 or 3 years to form strong roots.

# MOWING

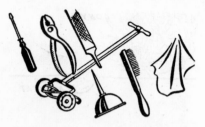

**1.** One of the first requirements for a successful lawn is the proper care of the mowing machine. Oil it regularly, and brush off and wipe the blades after each mowing. Keep pliers and screwdriver on hand for tightening loose bolts.

MOW COMPLETE LAWN IN DIRECTION A THEN-CROSS CUT (DIRECTION B)

**4.** A smooth, even-textured lawn is achieved by mowing the entire lawn in one direction, then mowing again at right angles to the first direction. The basket or grass catcher can be left off the mower during the second mowing. Let the mower overlap each strip a little, and thus avoid leaving narrow portions of uncut grass.

**2.** Leaves cut off light, water and air from grass. Before mowing, rake off leaves. A good device for use on large lawns is a curved pipe with a nozzle which forces water out in a very strong stream and drives the leaves in front of it.

**5.** New lawns are mowed when about 3″-4″ high. Set the mower blades at 2″, a safe height. It is important to roll new lawns the day before the first mowing. This firms in roots which might otherwise be pulled up by the mower blades.

**3.** Always weed before mowing. Some weeds, such as morning glory and dandelions, develop stronger root systems after having their tops cut off. After lifting out the weed, firmly tamp down the disturbed grass.

**6.** A well kept lawn should always have its edges cut with clippers or a small one-sided mower especially built for this purpose. Where grass has grown very high among trees or in a more natural setting, it can be cut with a sickle.

# PERENNIAL BORDERS

**1.** Perennial borders should be planned, prepared and planted as though they had come to stay. Double-digging (see Drainage) improves drainage, soil texture, adds food and air. Such digging, if well done, lasts 5 or 6 years.

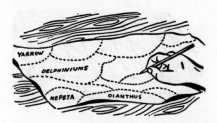

**4.** Plan your border on paper. Use graph paper, allowing 1 section per foot, or tracing paper, using a scale of ¼" or ½" to a foot. Books on perennial borders, magazine articles, and catalogues will help you make your plan.

**2.** Double-dig in the fall. If possible, the rough surface should be left to weather for 6 or 8 weeks. Wind, rain and frost will break up and crumble lumps and cause sinking of the border to the proper level.

**5.** Before planting, run a line along the front edge of the border, and place small stakes at 5' intervals just within the line. Divide the plan into corresponding 5' sections. You are now ready to work from the plan to the ground.

**3.** If rains fail to come early enough, water the border to cause settling. When it has dried out sufficiently, rake it to a fine tilth. The final level should be slightly higher than that of the surrounding ground.

**6.** Next gather necessary plant material together. Lift only those you need for the day's planting. Working from the plan, place plants in their positions in the first 5 or 10 feet, then plant. Groups should be long and tapering, for the most part.

# PERENNIALS

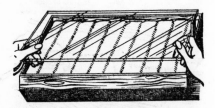

**1.** One of the advantages of perennials is the ease with which they are propagated. Seed sowing is usually the simplest method. Many perennials bloom the first year from seed (delphiniums, for instance); some require 2 years, a short time, considering the results.

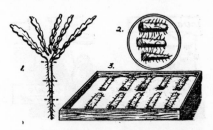

**4.** Tap-rooted plants are best propagated by root cuttings. Cut the roots (about the size of a pencil) into 1½" lengths. Place them horizontally in a flat filled with compost and cover to their own depth. Oriental poppy, windflower, verbascum, phlox and other plants can be propagated this way.

**2.** Dividing of perennials is done in the late fall and early winter. Wait until spring in cold districts. Agapanthus, aubrieta, arabis, campanula, daylily, dianthus, heuchera, gerbera, yarrow, salvia, and shasta daisies are some that can be propagated by division.

**5.** After cutting back certain perennials, such as dianthus and delphinium, place a mixture of sand, peat and a little commercial fertilizer around the plants. In a few weeks new shoots will appear. When these have become firm, take basal cuttings with a "heel," or with part of the old stock attached. Root in sand.

**3.** Many perennials, such as marguerite, pentstemon, verbena, dianthus, gypsophila, and eupatorium are easily propagated from cuttings. These are usually made from sideshoots in fall or in early spring, rooted in sand, potted up, and planted out after root systems are well established.

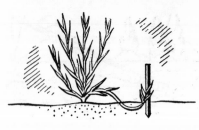

**6.** Perennials can also be layered (see Layering). Many procumbent plants, such as strawberry, cotoneaster, etc., layer themselves. Dianthus, pentstemon and verbena are among those that can be propagated by this method.

# PESTS

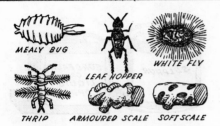

**1.** *Thrips* are small, slender, suck juices of fruit, foliage and flower. *Mealy bugs*, waxy and white, suck plant sap, excrete stickiness. *White flies* suck plant sap, excrete stickiness. *Scales* are hard shields under which the young scales live and suck plant juices. *Leafhoppers* are winged, spotted, suck plant juices and kill tissues.

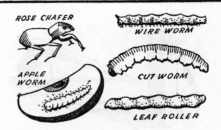

**4.** *Wireworms* live in soil and attack potatoes, beets, beans, asters, chrysanthemums. *Cutworms*, the larvae of night-flying insects, chew plants at the bottom of the stem. *Leafrollers* are caterpillars which attack leaves of apples, cherries. Kill *apple worms* when emerging from eggs. *Rose chafers* eat foliage.

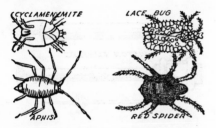

**2.** *Red spiders* suck juices and cause yellowing of leaves. *Cyclamen mites* are pale green, cause cyclamen leaves and buds to curl and become discolored. *Aphis* cause stickiness, and are cherished by ants. *Lace bugs* cause black, sticky conditions on the underside of Christmas Berry leaves.

**5.** *Snails, slugs, sowbugs* and *earwigs* lurk under rubbish piles and heavy-foliaged plants, especially when damp. The best control is a periodic cleaning up. Use poison baits in bad attacks; spread on dampened ground in the late afternoon or early evening.

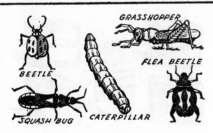

**3.** *Diabroticas* (12-spotted beetles) eat leaves and flowers; their larvae eat roots and tubers. *Caterpillars* chew foliage and become moths and butterflies. *Grasshoppers* attack flowers and vegetables. *Squash bugs* attack squash and melon plants. *Flea beetles* (shiny blue or green) eat leaves.

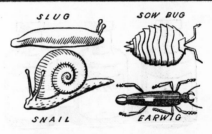

**6.** The regular control of ants is especially important, since they harbor and care for aphis, mealy bugs and scales. Gophers and moles must be watched especially in the spring and summer. Squirrels are not a problem except in the country districts; call your county agricultural commissioner if the problem is acute.

# PEST CONTROL

**1.** A hand sprayer of the piston type is sufficient for small gardens and greenhouses. Larger gardens will require a tank or compressed-air sprayer, usually holding about 3 gallons of spray. Select sprayers made of durable material. Clean after each using.

**4.** Fungous diseases, such as rust, leaf curl, blister or powdery mildew occur on many plants. Among bacterial diseases are blights, such as pear blight, and crown gall. The use of dusting sulphur, Bordeaux mixture, and mercury compounds helps to control these diseases.

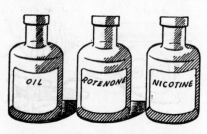

**2.** Sucking insects must be destroyed by a spray which will smother them by covering breathing pores. Sprays which contain a combination of oil and nicotine, rotenone, or pyrethrum are most effective. Several commercial preparations containing these ingredients are on the market.

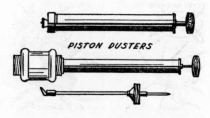

**5.** Piston dusters come in several sizes, designed to meet the needs of various sized gardens. An effective type is one shaped like a bellows, which disseminates the dusting powder so evenly and finely that no spore or bacteria often escapes.

**3.** Chewing or biting insects must be destroyed by a stomach poison which coats the plant with a thin covering. Sprays, dusts or baits containing lead arsenate, calcium arsenate, nicotine or fluorine give most effective control. Calcium and lead arsenate should be kept out of reach of children and pets.

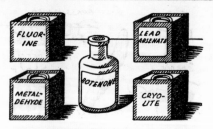

**6.** Chewing and biting insects are controlled by means of dusts and powders as well as by liquid sprays. Among the poisons used for this purpose are cryolite, fluorine and metaldehyde, the latter an ingredient in most of the newer and more effective baits for snails slugs and sowbugs.

# POTTING

SOIL  LEAF MOLD  SAND

POTS  BROKEN CROCKERY  LATH OR STICK

**1.** Before starting potting, gather all your materials together and see that the plants to be potted are moist. Old pots should be cleaned with a brush or with water. New pots should be thoroughly soaked before they are used.

**4.** If one finds an under-developed or little-developed root system, the plant should be replaced in the same pot. Never put a small plant in a large pot; the unused soil will become sour and the plant may suffer.

**2.** To remove properly a plant from a pot, turn the pot upside down, supporting the plant and holding in the soil with one hand. Then sharply tap one side of the pot on the edge of a table or bench.

WATER LEVEL

**5.** Pot most plants firmly to avoid drying out and to hold the plant upright. (Ferns, begonia and cineraria are some that can be potted more loosely). Use a lath or stick to firm the soil between the plant and the side of the pot. Soak plants in a bucket or water with a fine spray.

**3.** If a plant is "pot bound," some of the old, heavy roots should be cut back before potting on. This will stimulate new roots and make a better-balanced plant. Some plants, such as geraniums, like being slightly pot bound.

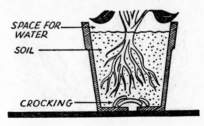

SPACE FOR WATER

SOIL

CROCKING

**6.** A properly potted plant should have: (1) Crock placed in an arching position over the drainage hole; (2) pebbles or smaller crocks; (3) if desired, a layer of sphagnum moss; (4) soil mixture, 3 loam, 1 leafmold, 1 sand. Leave 1″ at the top for watering.

# PRUNING

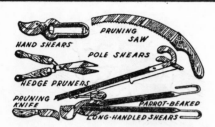

**1.** Pruning tools should always be kept clean and sharp. Carefully clean and wipe them before putting them away. During pruning operations on any shrub or tree which might be affected with blight, keep a disinfectant handy and apply to the pruning tool after each cut.

**4.** Prune evergreen hedges when new growth has become dark and stiff. The usual rule for shaping hedges, such as privet, pittosporum or yew, is to make them narrower at the top than at the bottom, so as to permit the entrance of sunlight and air to the lower portion of the hedge.

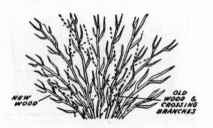

**2.** Shrubs that flower before June can be pruned immediately after flowering. Remove all old wood, crossing and weak branches, and suckers. The result should be a graceful, arching shrub with an open center. Flowering shrubs should never be topped in a straight, severe line.

**5.** In pruning, make a slanting cut, usually to an outside bud, which will later develop into an outward-pointing branch or stem. Placing the blades of the pruners in a line with the bud, make the cut about ¼″ above it. Avoid, if possible, leaving split wood.

**3.** Many broad-leaved evergreen shrubs, such as rhododendrons, are pruned by merely removing dead flower heads. Others, like escallonias, are pruned harder, their stems being cut back ⅓ to ½. It is best to cut to a green bud or leaf whenever possible.

**6.** Cut and undercut large branches to avoid splitting. Break the fall of heavy limbs with a rope. Tie one end to the limb to be cut, the other end to the trunk or a higher branch. Very heavy limbs need a prop underneath. Paint large wounds with a cauterizer as a preventive against decay or rot.

# SEED SOWING

**1.** Materials required are: Redwood flats; broken crocks, gravel or other drainage material; sifter, with a bottom of ½" wire mesh; compost (1 part of garden loam, 1 part leafmold, 1 part of sand. A mixture of ⅔ peat and ⅓ sand can also be used.) Sift compost, mix well, place in flats, pressing it firmly into the corners.

**4.** Write labels and place them at the head of the drills. Small sticks or green bamboo stakes can be used to separate drills containing different varieties. Mix small seed with a little fine sand before sowing—to see clearly where the seed falls.

**2.** For a smooth surface, level with wooden block, leaving ¼" of space between the soil and the top of the flat. To provide a very smooth surface for small seeds, such as primulas, an extra surface sifting of compost through a fine sieve is recommended.

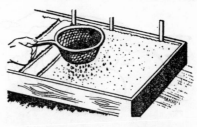

**5.** Cover the seed with the same compost to which extra sand has been added. Some prefer to use sand only. A good rule to follow is to cover to the depth of the seed itself. Extra fine seed should not be covered; merely press it gently into the soil with a flat, level piece of wood.

**3.** Using a short ruler or a straight-edged stick, make shallow drills 2" apart. If the seed to be sown is coarse, the drills can be quite deep (approximately ¼"). Sow fine seed in very shallow drills (⅛" or less).

**6.** Thoroughly water the flat with a fine over-, head spray or by soaking the flat in a large basin. Place it in a greenhouse or a warm spot not reached by direct sunlight. Cover with a glass and a double thickness of newspaper. Turn the glass each day to ventilate and remove excess moisture.

# SHRUBS (planting)

**1.** Preparation for the planting of shrubs should be thorough. Dig a much larger hole than the ball or root system of the shrub requires. Place topsoil to one side, subsoil to another. Break up the bottom of the hole. with a fork or pick.

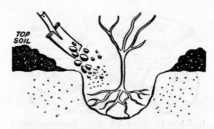

**4.** Roots of deciduous (bare-root) plants should be inspected for bruises or tears and pruned back beyond the injured point. Also prune tops. Then plant, carefully spreading the roots and gently filling in about them with topsoil. Set plants to same depth as they were in the nursery.

**2.** "Heel in," or place in a trench, with roots well covered, all bare-root material and balled trees and shrubs when they arrive from the nursery. Occasionally trees or shrubs with bare roots are so dry that soaking in water previous to planting is advisable. Water those in containers 1 or 2 days prior to planting.

**5.** After the soil has been filled in around the roots, tamp down the surface with the ball of the foot. Leave a basin 6" deep around the trunk or stem of the plant. This insures ample water; it can later be filled in. If planting a tree, stake it against winds.

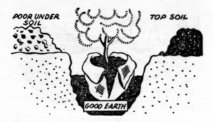

**3.** Before planting, fill in the bottom of the hole with good soil. Carefully handle balled plants so as not to break the ball. If the ball is very firm, cut the twine holding the burlap. Next fill in with topsoil, pressing it in well about the ball. The burlap will soon rot away.

**6.** Water regularly all newly planted material. In autumn or winter, rains will probably come on to help solve the watering problem; in spring, especially after planting evergreens, both surface and overhead watering may be necessary. Feed with commercial fertilizer after shrubs are established.

# SHRUBS AND TREES (moving)

**1.** The moving of all but very small trees and shrubs requires skill and care. One year before actual moving is to take place, preferably in early spring, dig a trench 3′ deep and 18″ wide, 3′ to 5′ away from the trunk, depending on the size of the tree.

**4.** Before or immediately after planting, cut back the top of the tree ¼ or ⅓. This will reduce the amount of transpiration, or the escape of water vapor through the leaves, and so reduce the amount of shock on the tree.

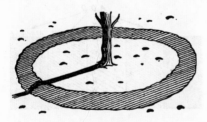

**2.** Cut with an axe or heavy pruning shears all roots passing through the trench. Fill in the trench with ¾ topsoil and ¼ manure and water thoroughly. This will stimulate new feeder roots in the trench or nearer the trunk.

**5.** Plant in a large hole and fill in with loose, rich topsoil, carefully firming the soil around the roots. Make a large basin around the trunk and slowly soak with water. Spray overhead with water, also.

**3.** One year later the tree will be ready for moving. Again dig around the trench, this time with a spading fork, and carefully uncover the roots. Burlap, canvas or other material should be used to cover the roots and keep them from drying out.

**6.** Guy wires prevent shifting of the tree during heavy winds. Three wires, placed 120° apart, equalize the tension. Girdling of branches by wires is best prevented by inserting 3 wooden blocks between the bark and wire. Ample light and air are thus available to the bark.

# SOILS

**1.** Soils contain minerals, derived from rocks that have been weathered and broken down through the ages. Weathering is effected by mechanical action (rain, wind, wave and stream action, heat and cold, and roots of plants); by chemical action of water, oxygen and carbon dioxide in the air.

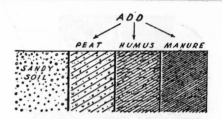

**4.** Sandy soil, composed of large particles which readily fall apart, has large pore spaces. Though actually heavy because of the weight of the individual particles, it is called light because it is easily worked. Add humus, peat and manure to improve moisture-holding capacity, texture and to add food.

**2.** Soils also contain organic matter, formed by the remains of plants and animals deposited under water and in a state of decomposition. Peat, which is the best known form of organic matter, is vegetable matter in an arrested state of decay.

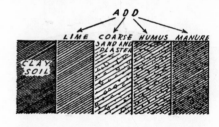

**5.** Clay is composed of small particles which adhere closely together, forming a plastic, tenacious mass. Lighter than sand, it is called heavy because it is hard to work. Improve it by working and adding lime, sand, plaster, humus and manure.

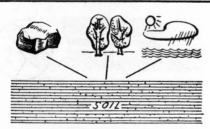

**3.** Besides minerals and organic matter, soil contains a varying amount of water. Between the particles of organic and mineral matter are pore spaces. If these spaces are largely filled with water, the soil will be boggy and mucky; if with air, a loamy, or better balanced soil.

**6.** There are many types of loam, varying from light and sandy to heavy and clayey types. The ideal loam is a fertile soil containing sand, clay and humus in the proper proportions. Neither too light nor too heavy, it is the type of soil all gardeners work to achieve.

# SOIL TESTING

**1.** Most soil-testing methods are quite complicated. A simple, though not very sensitive test can be made with litmus, obtainable in any drugstore. Soil to be tested should be moist. If it is predominantly acid, the litmus paper will turn red; if alkaline, the paper will remain blue.

**4.** One can also judge soils by the type of vegetation present. Moss, sorrel, a strong growth of foxgloves, bracken fern, or of any other plant thriving in acid soil indicates acidity. On the other hand, lush growth of clover or alfalfa indicates a sweet soil.

**2.** Soils can be tested for acidity or alkalinity by means of chemical indicators or solutions. A pinch of soil is placed in the large well on the porcelain plate. Enough indicator is dropped on the soil sample to moisten it thoroughly. Let it stand 3 or 4 minutes.

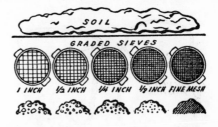

**5.** Soils are tested to ascertain the size of the particles and the relative amount of clay and sand. A set of sieves with trays at the bottom is used. Soil is passed through the sieves and weighed. Anything over 1/8" in diameter is considered stone.

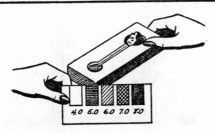

**3.** Incline the plate to allow the solution to pass from the large to the small well. Next compare the color of the solution with the colored bands on the pH card to learn the degree of acidity present. 7.0 is the symbol for a neutral soil.

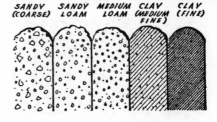

**6.** If a large proportion of sand is found in soil, it is considered poor and will require the addition of clay, manure, humus and other coarse materials. A large proportion of clay indicates a heavy soil. Midway between sand and clay is loam, the ideal soil.

# STAKING

**1.** Staking is required by weak-stemmed and top-heavy plants; by tall plants with leafless flowering stems; and by long-stemmed cutflowers. Redwood stakes should be treated at the bottom with creosote. Various metal stakes or plant supports are commercially available. The "crutch" type (E) is good support for delicate or brittle-stemmed plants.

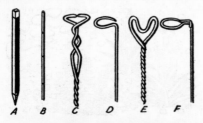

**2.** These two metal stakes can be used either in the garden or for pot plants. Plants are held upright, but not so tightly that the natural shape is destroyed. An extension at the bottom allows the stakes to be more firmly inserted.

**3.** Cutflowers, such as chrysanthemum, shasta daisy or hardy aster are best grown in rows. Stake them as illustrated. Drive 3'-4' redwood stakes at 6' intervals on either side of the row; stretch wire between the stakes (2 to 3 rows of wire will be needed).

**4.** Large, wide-spreading plants, such as peony or gypsophila, can be held within bounds by encircling them with chicken wire. As the plants grow, the wire becomes concealed and is finally covered. Early staking is especially necessary in this case.

**5.** Large plants can be supported by encircling them with 2 or 3 rows of raffia tied to 3 or 4 well placed stakes. Another method is that of placing a strong stake in the center of the clump, and of tieing each stem separately to this stake.

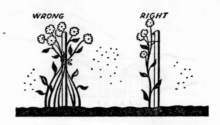

**6.** A favorite method of staking among amateurs seems to be that of tieing in large plants to a single stake so that they resemble hour glass figures. To retain the natural shape of a plant, tie each stem separately or enclose the plant loosely.

# TOOLS AND WORKSHOP

**1.** Tools have special uses. The spading fork with long tines is best for digging in heavy soil, the spade for rough digging, the shovel for moving soil, spreading manure, as well as for digging, while the small (ladies') fork is good for light digging.

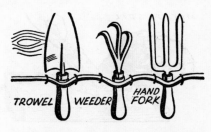

**4.** Clothesline rope and some staples are all that are needed to make this simple holder for small tools. Each tool has its special place with its name lettered below so as to avoid mix-ups. Keep an oiled rag nearby.

**2.** A steel rake for leveling and smoothing the ground, a hoe for weeding and cultivating, a small cultivator for fine work, a trowel, and a bamboo rake complete the list of tools every gardener should own. Clean and wipe them with an oiled rag after using.

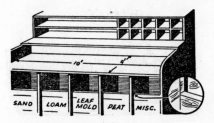

**5.** This potting bench is long and wide enough to accommodate bins beneath for soil and other potting materials. Removable slats in front allow easy access to a diminishing supply. The small compartments are for brushes, dibbers, labels and other parts of the gardener's equipment.

**3.** The sight of shining, well cared for tools warms a gardener's heart. Metal tool holders, offered commercially, enable one to arrange tools compactly, neatly and with little waste space. Wooden rods, or pegs, placed as in the diagram, are also satisfactory.

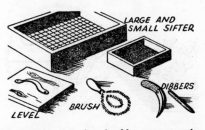

**6.** These accessories should accompany the potting bench: ¼" and ½" mesh sifters for soil, leafmold and peat; a fine sifter for seed covering; a wooden level for seed flats; a brush for cleaning pots and boxes; and dibbers for pricking out.

# TRANSPLANTING SEEDLINGS

*MIXED SOIL*

**1.** The operation of transplanting seedlings is called "pricking out." The initial preparation of the flat is the same as for seed sowing. The compost or soil mixture contains 2 parts of good garden loam, 1 part leafmold, 1 part sand and ½ part peat.

**4.** After pricking out a flat of seedlings, water immediately with a fine spray to settle the soil around the roots and to freshen wilted stems and leaves. A watering can is better than a hose.

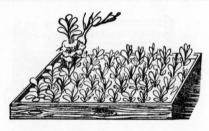

**2.** Seedlings are ready to prick out when they have 2 pairs of leaves. Sprinkle them a short time before pricking out with Vitamin B-I solution to reduce shock from moving. Lift seedlings from the seed flat with a fork and gently separate them. Most seedlings should be pricked out 2″ apart each way.

**5.** If the seed box from which the seedlings have been taken has been in the greenhouse, the newly pricked out flat should be placed in the greenhouse. Cover with a sheet of newspaper from 3 to 4 days, or until the seedlings have stiffened up.

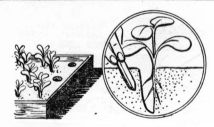

**3.** Working quickly, insert individual seedlings in the holes and firm them in with a dibber or one's fingertips. Keep the point of the dibber at least ½″ away from the delicate roots. Work in shade and out of drying winds or drafts.

**6.** In about 4 or 5 weeks, the young plants will be ready to go out into the open ground. A few days before planting, move the flats into the open to harden off. Nip back spindly plants to encourage bushiness.

# VITAMIN B-1

**1.** Vitamin B-1 is a chemical substance promoting root growth after the appearance of root primordia (buds at the base of cuttings from which roots spring). All plants manufacture Vitamin B-1, but very few produce enough to satisfy their needs. It is widely used for cuttings.

**4.** An important use of Vitamin B-1 is in transplanting large trees and shrubs. Ordinarily the shock of moving is great and roots are slow in re-establishing themselves. It has been possible through Vitamin B-1 to prevent setbacks and in some cases complete loss.

**2.** Vitamin B-1 is not a fertilizer, though it does increase a plant's capacity for food by enlarging the root system. If food is present in the soil, the plant treated with Vitamin B-1 will absorb more than the untreated plant.

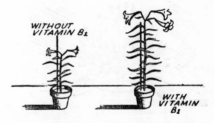

WITHOUT VITAMIN $B_1$

WITH VITAMIN $B_1$

**5.** Potted plants as well as those growing in the open ground have shown remarkable results after being treated with Vitamin B-1. Azaleas, camellias, gardenias, cyclamen and primulas have increased in vigor and produced larger and earlier blooms.

**3.** Approximately 8 drops of liquid Vitamin B-1 are needed to make one gallon of solution. If using the powder, the amount one can get on the end of a toothpick is sufficient, after being dissolved in water, to make several gallons of solution. Read directions carefully.

**6.** Transplanted seedlings suffer a certain amount of shock. A disturbed root system, resulting in a decreased absorption of water and a consequent drying out of leaves, causes frequent loss. Water with Vitamin B-1 before and after transplanting to prevent this loss.

# WATERING

**1.** Flooding is the best method of watering borders containing flowered, tall-stemmed plants that are apt to be broken down by an overhead spray. Tie a piece of sack over the end of a hose, and allow the water to flow evenly and gently through the bed.

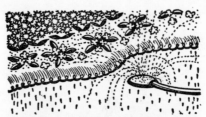

**4.** Overhead sprinkling is best for lawns, large flower beds with fairly low planting, and for such plants as cinerarias, tuberous and fibrous begonias, ferns and fuchsias. A fine spray will not break brittle stems or weak-headed flowers. Overhead sprinkling helps to discourage such pests as red spider, aphis, scale and mealybug.

**2.** Roses become mildewed when watered overhead. To avoid this, as well as discoloration of blooms, water them by flooding in basins around the base of each bush. Later fill the basin with loose soil to form a mulch and prevent drying out.

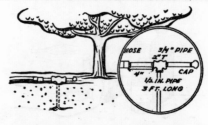

**5.** Large trees and shrubs, newly planted or well established, occasionally need special watering. Water from overhead sprinkling is usually dissipated before reaching the lower root system. The watering pipe illustrated overcomes this deficiency. Plunge it into the ground at various points within 3'-6' from the trunk and soak slowly and long.

**3.** Cutflowers, vegetables, strawberries, etc., are best watered by the furrow method. With a hoe, make a V-shaped furrow between rows. Allow the water to run very slowly from a hose until the furrow is full and the hills between furrows entirely soaked.

**6.** Large potted ferns, palms, and other large-balled plants cannot always be watered satisfactorily from above. Give them a weekly or twice-monthly soaking by standing them in their pots in a bucket of water. Allow them to remain until the ball has become saturated.

# WEEDS

**1.** Control weeds in their early stages. In time, perennial weeds root more firmly and deeply; annual weeds seed and propagate themselves anew. Morning glory (1) and dandelion (4), common weed pests, deserve special attention. Mallow (2) (sometimes called cheeses) seeds persistently, as does milkweed (3).

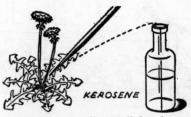

**4.** Kerosene or gasoline, applied to the center of dandelion plants with a pointed stick or nail will kill the weed. Heavy doses of ammonium sulphate will also, in time, destroy dandelions. On lawns, ammonium sulphate will serve as a fertilizer as well, though the surrounding grass may look a little yellow for a few days.

**2.** Plantain (1), a common lawn weed, can be hand weeded or destroyed with caustic soda, carbolic acid or iron sulfate. Crab grass (3) must be pulled out before it seeds in early summer. Sheep's sorrel (4), found in sour soil, and many-rooted chickweed (2) can be killed with iron sulfate.

**5.** Wild morning glory is one of the most destructive of weeds. Its roots extend from 7'-30' feet into the ground. The smallest piece of root can originate a new plant. Spraying with sodium chloride, chloride of arsenic, or caustic soda is effective; so is repeated cutting under the ground.

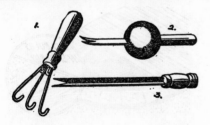

**3.** A common weeder is the pronged type with a knot (2), used to tamp down disturbed ground after removal of the weed. The curved, fingered weeder (1) can be used for cultivating, also. The best dandelion weeder is one (3) with sharp, tapered points and concaved edges which enclose the taproot.

**6.** Constant cultivation, especially before seeding time, is the best control for both annual and perennial weeds. A shuffle hoe or an ordinary garden hoe are good for this purpose. If possible, cut out perennial weeds by the roots.

# WINTER STORAGE

**1.** Thrips are the worst enemies of gladiolus. Here is the best method of control. After the corms have been lifted and cleaned, store them, labeled, in paper bags and sprinkle naphthalene flakes over them. Tie tops of the bags tightly, store them in a cool, dry, well-ventilated place.

**4.** Perforated baking powder or spice cans make dry, rodent-proof seed containers. A long, narrow box, shaped like a shoe box, with 12 divisions for the calendar year, is also good. Labeled seed packets are filed away according to the month they should be sown.

**2.** After the tops of tuberous begonias have yellowed, dry and clean tubers and place in flats of dry sand or peat. If stacking the flats, place wedges between them to allow free circulation of air. A garage, basement or shed is a good storage place.

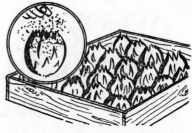

**5.** Lilies should not be kept out of the ground longer than necessary. If one must store lilies, dust them with sulphur, especially in the spaces between the scales. Shippers often pack them in dry peat moss; they can be stored in the same manner.

**3.** Sun-dry lifted dahlia clumps for a week, then cut back the tops to 1″ or 2″ and dust the hollow stumps with sulphur to prevent rot. If stored in a furnace-heated basement, cover with sand, peat or burlap to prevent shrinkage.

**6.** In cold districts, it is best to drain lily pools or cover them with boards, topped with a layer of straw. Otherwise, remove the lilies and store in a box of moist sand. To insure against dry-rot, keep them covered with moist burlap.

# ANNUALS

We have by no means attempted to rival the seed catalogues in listing annuals — we have tried to present as much information as possible on those annuals which have been found most practical and adaptable for a wide variety of uses, and whose flowering periods, together, form a continuous succession of bloom. When any basic operation is referred to, you will find it explained in detail in the "Garden Techniques" section (page 3). If, for any plant, this technique should be varied, the special culture needed is described under the name of the plant.

# ASTER

**1.** The true name of the annual or garden aster is Callistephus (Greek for beautiful crown). A native of China and Japan, it was originally a hairy-leaved plant with one flower on a single stalk. Grow only wilt-resistant strains. The Crego type is one of the best.

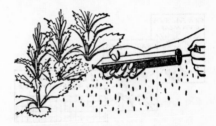

**4.** A short time before the plants are ready to set out, lightly fork the ground once more and rake it to a fine tilth. When the plants are 4″ high, plant them 1′ apart in an open, sunny bed.

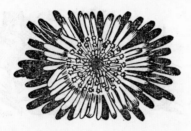

WOOD ASH    MANURE

**2.** The preparation of soil for asters is an important factor in their successful growing. Two months before planting, deeply spade or fork the ground and work in a generous amount of rich, well-rotted cow manure. Woodash is also beneficial.

**5.** Asters are attacked by various diseases and pests, including wilt, mildew, rust, yellows, aphis and stem borers. Wilt-resistant strains only should be grown; Bordeaux mixture and sulphur will help to control diseases; nicotine and arsenical sprays and dusts should be used for pests.

SOW MAR.-MAY

**3.** For early bloom, one must start asters indoors. Do not sow them too thickly, since they are, like many seedlings, susceptible to damping off. After danger of frosts is over, one can sow them directly in the ground where they are to bloom.

PLANT FOOD

**6.** Water thoroughly, but not too often, and always follow up with cultivation. When buds appear, though before they show color, feed plants with commercial fertilizer (about 1 tablespoon to a plant), which must be watered in immediately afterward.

# CENTAUREA

**1.** Two of the best-known annual centaureas are *C. cyanus* (cornflower or Bachelor's Button) and *C. moschata* (Sweet Sultan). Cornflowers come in shades of blue, pink, white, mauve, and ruby. Sweet Sultan comes in the same colors with the addition of yellow.

**4.** Sow centaureas directly in rows for cutting purposes. They need not be thinned a great deal, for centaureas like being crowded. Cornflowers are, as a rule, sprawly in habit; grown thickly, they hold each other up.

**2.** Centaureas are hardy and are best when grown from fall-sown seed. This applies to both California and the Pacific Northwest, where they can be sown in September or October and get well started before cold weather sets in.

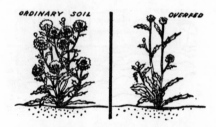

**5.** Unlike most flowers, both cornflowers and Sweet Sultans dislike rich soil or food. Natives of rather poor soil, they flower best when not treated too well. Feeding tends to develop vegetative growth and retard flowering.

**3.** Centaureas are best sown in the ground where they are to remain, for they transplant rather badly. They like an open, sunny position and a light, not too rich, well-drained soil. No manure need be added. After sowing, cover the seed with peat and keep it moist until after the seedlings appear.

**6.** The special, or traditional use of the cornflower is as a cutflower. And nowhere does it seem more fitting than in a man's coat lapel. Both cornflowers and Sweet Sultans belong in the old-fashioned garden and in the old-fashioned bouquet.

# CINERARIA

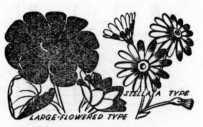

1. Cinerarias are among the most beautiful of winter and spring-flowering plants. The two main types are the large-flowered and the stellata or star cineraria. Both are used as bedding and as pot plants for shady locations.

4. Aside from shade and light, leafy soil, the cineraria enjoys plenty of water, especially sprinkling on its leaves on warm days. Cinerarias combine well with ferns, rhododendrons, azaleas, fuchsias, hydrangeas, primroses, lilies, hellebores and other shade-loving shrubs and plants.

2. Seed of cinerarias can be sown from May to October. Always grow them under cool conditions. During the summer it will be necessary to give them special care (watering, shading, etc.). A lathhouse is an ideal place in which to summer them.

5. Cinerarias are especially well adapted to pot culture. They should be grown under cool conditions, with the day temperature kept down to 60°, and the night to 50°. For fall and winter bloom, start from seed in May, prick out in June, pot up in July.

3. Cinerarias thrive in light, leafy, cool soil. Ground under pines, oaks, redwoods, or other trees growing in slightly acid conditions will suit their needs. If the soil has not previously been prepared, add leafmold, peat, and woodash and sand if the soil is inclined to heaviness.

6. Pot on cinerarias as they become pot bound. They should flower in 6"-8" pots. When the plants set buds, feed once weekly with weak liquid manure (made by submerging a sack of manure in a barrel or tub of water). Discontinue feeding when in flower.

# DIMORPHOTHECA

**1.** The common name of the dimorphotheca is cape marigold. It is a native of South Africa and thrives in sun and a light soil, just as does another South African flower, the Transvaal daisy, or gerbera.

**2.** Dimorphothecas are particularly good for winter work. To have them in bloom in winter, sow the seed in August. One can start them either in boxes or broadcast in the open ground.

**3.** As a winter or spring annual border, dimorphothecas can hardly be surpassed. A good medium height, not over 12"-15" high, they are literally covered with daisylike flowers in shades of yellow, orange, salmon and white. They bloom for at least 3 months.

**4.** If growing them as pot plants, give them an ordinary potting compost (3 parts loam, 1 part leafmold, 1 part sand); put one plant in a 4" or 5" pot, or 3 plants in a 7" pot. Give them cool treatment in a greenhouse or a frame. Feed with weak liquid manure when the plants set buds.

**5.** A sunny, well drained rock garden is an ideal spot for drifts or clumps of dimorphothecas. They are especially effective in fairly broad masses of one color and are helpful as fillers in a new rock garden in which small, slow-growing plants have not yet made much effect.

**6.** Dimorphothecas make bright flower arrangements, also. While they close up at night and on dark days, they open in sunlight and last well indoors. An especially lovely dimorphotheca is the variety Glistening White.

# GODETIA

**1.** Godetias are among the more unusual garden annuals to which new colors and improved forms are being added. Their rich colors are heightened by a satiny texture. They bloom from early spring to summer and make excellent, long-lasting cutflowers.

**4.** Godetias are one of the best annual fillers for perennial borders. Their height, 18"-24", is a good intermediate one, and they combine well with many plants. They come in a beautiful white, a salmon-pink, a deep salmon-orange, carmine and rosy-pink.

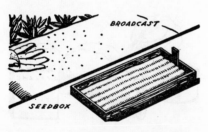

**2.** Godetias can be started indoors in flats or broadcast in the open ground. Since they seem to enjoy cool culture, the fall and early spring are the seasons for starting them. Grow them on fast; plant them out before they become woody.

**5.** Massed in the annual border, godetias make a striking display. Grow them along with other annuals requiring similar conditions. Especially attractive are the varieties Sybil Sherwood and Kelvedon Glory.

**3.** A sunny or half-shady location, in ordinary soil, is good for godetias. Set plants out 9"-10" apart or, if one is thinning them out in the place where sown, let them remain rather closely together, since they enjoy being crowded.

**6.** Godetias are among the most satisfactory cutflowers as to color, habit and lasting qualities. Grown in well drained, not rich soil, they will give profuse bloom over a long period. A glistening pure white variety, sometimes called White Swan, also Purity, is extraordinarily beautiful, as are some others.

# GOURDS

**1.** Gourds belong to the cucumber family, in which are also included pumpkins, squashes and melons. Being tropical in origin, they thrive only with heat, moisture and rich soil. All are tendril-bearing vines which, if unsupported, will sprawl on the ground.

**4.** If one intends to use gourds for decoration or in arrangements, they must be thoroughly ripened and ready to fall from the vine before being picked. Sun-cure for a few days, then scrub clean, rinse and wipe completely dry.

**2.** After all danger of frost is past, plant gourds in a sunny position against a fence or trellis, or near pergola or arbor posts. Make a large hole, place 6″ of manure in the bottom, fill with topsoil and plant 3 or 4 seeds (points down) in each hole.

**5.** Clean and dry, the gourds may be painted with clear shellac, applied with even strokes. If one carefully tacks staples in the tops of the gourds, it is possible to suspend them from a line and thus dry them without marring the shellacked surface.

**3.** Though gourds do not transplant easily, it is possible to sow seed in small pots and to set out the plants when they have 3 or 4 sets of leaves. Gourds make a quick, shade-giving, decorative covering for arbors and pergolas.

**6.** Gourds, with their varied, interesting and sometimes grotesque shapes, are excellent subjects for decoration, especially in autumn and winter. They can be used alone or in combination with ornamental corn, colored leaves, berries or autumnal flowers.

# LARKSPUR

**1.** Larkspurs, or annual delphiniums, have a grace of form that makes them especially useful as cutflowers or for planting in the border. They are frequently used in place of perennial delphinium when that plant is not available, and may be had in white and in pink, rose, and blue or lavender shades.

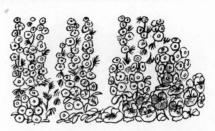

**4.** The graceful spikes of larkspurs make them especially valuable for mixed borders. Plant them in fairly solid masses in the middle of the border with a lower, bushier planting of such flowers as godetia in the foreground.

**2.** Larkspurs are most successful when grown under cool conditions. Fall-sown seed, either in flats or broadcast in the open ground, will produce spring flowers. Spring-sown seed, if started early, will give flowers up until the hot weather.

**5.** Larkspurs are susceptible to powdery mildew. It usually appears toward the end of the season; early planting and watering from below are probably the best preventives. Spraying with Bordeaux or sulphur may help to keep it under control, but will not entirely cure it.

**3.** In districts where warm spring weather prevails, plant or sow larkspurs in partially shaded positions. If grown as cutflowers, they can be seeded in trenches in the open ground and thinned out to 1'. Prepare the soil to a fine tilth. Manure should be added well in advance of planting.

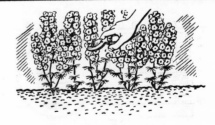

**6.** Cutting and removing seedpods will help to lengthen their period of bloom. Some staking may be required in the cutting garden. Growing them close together helps somewhat to hold them upright.

# MORNING GLORY

**1.** Morning glories are among our showiest annual vines. The most beautiful is the variety Heavenly Blue. There is also a white variety which blooms at night and on dull days, and is fragrant. Morning glories sown in March will bloom from June or early July until November.

**4.** Morning glories are fast growing, and will easily cover fences, trellises, arbors, pergolas, and walls. They can be grown in combination with other annual vines, such as *Mina lobata*, or with the perennial morning glory, *Ipomoea Learii.*

**2.** The seeds of morning glories and moon-flowers are vẽry hard coated. To facilitate germination, soak the seeds in warm water for a few hours or notch them with a file, knife or razor blade.

**5.** The Imperial Japanese morning glories are large flowered, brightly colored types which are frequently grown in large pots or tubs. One can also grow the annuals in pots or boxes and use them as hanging vines from a high wall or balcony.

**3.** In late March or early April, after the ground has become warmed, plant seeds in loose, well prepared soil. Do not add manure, since annual morning glories grow best in ordinary soil. They can also be started indoors in pots and planted out later.

**6.** Frequently a quick covering is needed to cover large bare spaces on newly built houses, garages or sheds. Winter-blooming vines sometimes need a summer-flowering complement. Morning glories are among the loveliest climbers for this purpose.

# PANSY

**1.** Pansies are perennials, but are treated as annuals and are grown from seed each year. One of their ancestors is the Heart's Ease or wild pansy, a native of Europe but found wild in most countries. Pansies have a wide number of uses in the garden.

**4.** The less pansies are transplanted the larger their blooms will be. Keep plenty of soil around the roots when moving them from the flat and place a trowelful of moist peat in each hole before planting. Plant pansies 9″ apart. Mulch them during warm weather.

**2.** When growing pansies, select the best strains from a reliable seed house. It is best to use fresh seed; old seed, unless kept over in glass jars in a refrigerator, germinates unevenly. Sow in August; never allow young seedlings to dry out, for pansies lack the vitality to revive, once they have become very dry.

**5.** From the time buds appear until plants are in full bloom, feed every 2 weeks with a commercial fertilizer or with liquid manure. The color of pansies is improved by the use of soot water, a solution made with chimney soot.

**3.** The soil for pansies can hardly be too rich. Four to 6 weeks in advance of planting, deeply dig and manure the ground. Do not plant pansies where they will get the mid-day sun, since this shortens their season and fades their blooms.

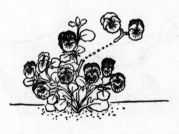

**6.** To lengthen the blooming period of pansies, pick them frequently and keep seed pods removed. Never allow them to dry out. Water generously, especially at the end of warm days.

# PETUNIA

**1.** Perhaps there is no better known or more widely used annual than the petunia. It is a member of the nightshade or potato family and is a native of the Argentine. Hybridizers are constantly introducing new petunias, including ruffled, fringed, double and single types.

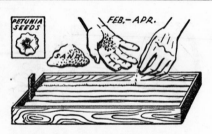

**2.** Petunias are usually propagated by seed. Double, ruffled and fringed forms can be increased by cuttings. Petunia seed is very fine, and should not be covered. Mix it with fine sand and gently press it into the seed compost with a block of wood.

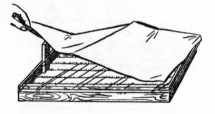

**3.** The seed compost for petunias must be light and leafy and kept fairly moist. After sowing, cover with glass and a sheet of newspaper. Lift and turn the glass each day. Prick out the seedlings when the second pair of leaves have developed.

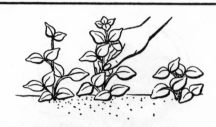

**4.** When the plants are 6" high, pinch them back to encourage lateral growth. This will defer flowering a few weeks, but a sturdier, longer-blooming plant will result. When picking petunias, remove some of the foliage along with the flowers.

**5.** Two or 3 days after watering, cultivate petunia beds, leaving a fine mulch over the surface of the soil. Feed with commercial fertilizer (1 teaspoon to a plant) once a month up until plants are in full bloom. Water after feeding.

**6.** Aside from their usefulness as bedding plants, petunias make excellent pot plants, giving color to terraces, patios and porches from early summer to late fall. Balcony petunias, available in a wide range of colors, are standbys for sunny window boxes.

# PHLOX DRUMMONDI

**1.** From Texas comes the original form of *Phlox drummondi*, also called Texan Pride. For beauty of coloring and suitability for bedding and cutting, it is hardly surpassed by any other annual. Seed of new varieties, such as the Art Shades, and separate colors, are sold in seed stores.

ANNUAL BORDER

**4.** Another way in which annual phlox can be used is in annual mixed borders. The wide variety of colors and delicate shadings make it possible to combine phlox with many other annuals. They are especially lovely when used with ageratum, low petunias, *Salvia farinacea*, and dwarf zinnias.

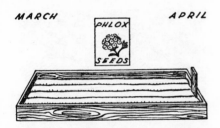

MARCH      APRIL

PHLOX SEEDS

**2.** Seed is sown in early spring in a cool greenhouse or coldframe. It is possible to sow them in the open ground in March or April. Keep them carefully shaded and watered during their early stages.

PERENNIAL BORDER

**5.** Phlox also make good fillers for perennial borders, where medium-height, late-season plants, especially those in pastel shades, are so often needed. They can be planted in empty spaces reserved for them or between plants that bloomed earlier and have been cut back.

**3.** Phlox are at their best when planted rather thickly in solid masses of 1 color or closely harmonized shades. They lend themselves well to planting in formal beds near the house, along paths or along the edges of lawns.

**6.** Annual phlox are among our most satisfactory cutflowers in late summer and fall, when other flowers become scarce. If containers are kept filled with fresh water, phlox will last at least 1 week in the house.

# SALPIGLOSSIS

**1.** Salpiglossis, or Painted Tongue, is, oddly enough, a member of the potato family, and comes from Chile. The flowers are shaped like petunias and the plants usually grow from 18″ to 30″ high. The lower type is best for bedding, the taller for cutting.

**4.** When used in formal beds, salpiglossis can be planted quite thickly, or about 9″ apart. This enables the plants to hold each other erect and also helps prevent excessive drying out or cracking of the soil. They combine well with petunias, zinnias and marigolds.

**2.** Grow from seed sown either in flats or where the plants are to bloom. It is best to start them early and to have them well established before hot weather. The seed is very fine, and can be covered very little or not at all. Cover outdoor sowings until germinated.

**5.** If sown later, salpiglossis will bloom until the frosts. If grown for cut flowers, plant them in rows 12″ apart and water them once weekly by the furrow method (see Watering). Cut frequently and remove faded blooms to keep them blooming longer.

**3.** Give salpiglossis a sunny, well-drained position. Plant them out when they are 4″ high. Once they are well established, only moderate watering is necessary, for salpiglossis are warm-country plants.

**6.** Rich, deep color tones and unusual veining give salpiglossis particular value for arrangements. Few flowers have the velvety reds, browns, yellows, purples and violet found in the better strains of salpiglossis. They are especially beautiful in copper, brass and wooden containers.

# SNAPDRAGON

**1.** Snapdragons come in tall, intermediate and dwarf forms that can be used for bedding, cut flowers, in mixed borders and rock gardens. Their long period of bloom, wide range of colors and spiky form give them especial value for artistic effects in house and garden.

**2.** Sow snapdragon seed in late summer or early fall in temperate regions, in early spring where freezing temperatures prevail. Rust, a fungous disease which attacks snapdragons, is best prevented by good culture. Grow them on rapidly and vigorously; allow no checking from drying out, and do not overwater.

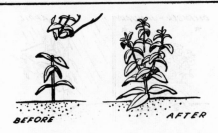

BEFORE          AFTER

**3.** Snapdragons tend to become leggy or spindly unless pinched back when they are about 6" high. Plants that are pinched back may be slightly retarded in blooming, but will reward with prolific and longer period of bloom.

**4.** If, after they have been planted out for some time, snapdragons seem to lag, feed them with a liquid fertilizer. Liquid cow manure is always safe, but a weak solution of sulphate of ammonia (1 tablespoon to 1 gallon of water) is also effective and very quick-acting. The soil about the plants should be moist before feeding.

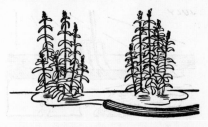

**5.** Watering from below is more effective than overhead sprinkling. It also lessens the danger of rust, spores of which disease are transmitted by means of water, wind or by insects. Water in the early part of the day or early evening, not in full sun.

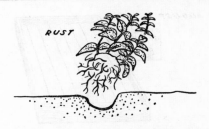

RUST

**6.** Until 100% rust-proof snapdragons are developed, careful treatment of seedlings and growing plants will prove the best preventive. Once the disease appears, remove and burn badly affected plants. Do not plant snapdragons in the same place year after year.

# STOCK

**1.** The gillyflower, as stock was once popularly called, was a favorite in American Colonial gardens. This inconspicuous, though spicily fragrant flower has come a long way since then. One may now have stock in tall, or dwarf, winter, spring or summer-flowering forms and in many beautiful shades.

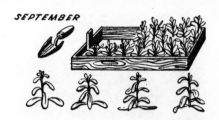

SEPTEMBER

**4.** If bushy, many-branched plants are desired, pinch back the main stems when the plants are about 6" high. If, on the other hand, large specimen flower stalks are preferred, remove the sideshoots. For the best results, stock must be grown without check.

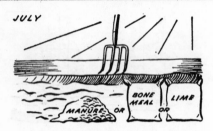

JULY

**2.** The ground for stock should be prepared several weeks ahead. Never use fresh manure. Stocks like sweet soil; a dressing of lime or gypsum well in advance of planting is beneficial. Liming every second or third year is sufficient. Drainage must be perfect.

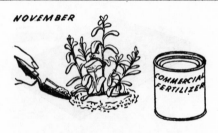

NOVEMBER

**5.** About once a month, up until the time the buds show color, feed stock with liquid manure or a balanced fertilizer. A mixture of blood and bonemeal, which gives both quick-acting and slow-acting results, is recommended by some growers.

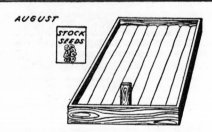

AUGUST

**3.** In warm climates, stock is successfully grown from July or August-sown seed and planted out while the ground is still warm. It will then bloom in winter and early spring. Where winters are severe, plant it out in spring after frosts are over.

DECEMBER — JANUARY       APRIL

**6.** Stock which has bloomed through the winter months will have passed its prime by late April and should be removed to make room for another crop. Where stock is grown as a spring or early summer flower, it can be depended upon until hot weather comes on.

# SWEET PEA

**1.** The original sweet pea, a little purple flower and a Sicilian native, was brought to England by a monk in 1699. The popular Spencer type, from which come our modern forms, originated as a "sport" in 1901 in the garden of the Earl of Spencer.

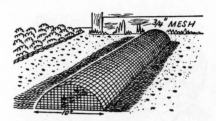

**4.** Thin crowded seedlings to 6", cover with wire or thin muslin as a protection from birds, and scatter snail bait. When plants are an inch or more high, fill in the drill to give young stems extra support.

**2.** Sweet peas can be planted from late summer to early spring. Remove topsoil to the depth of 18" and turn under 6" of manure in the bottom of the trench. Replace the topsoil, and work in bonemeal or gypsum (2 lbs. to 10').

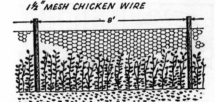

**5.** Stake sweet peas as soon as tendrils appear, using wire mesh, strong twine, or twiggy brush. Some growers pinch plants when they are 6" high to encourage sideshoots, which are later thinned. For specimen flowers, allow 2-3 shoots to a plant.

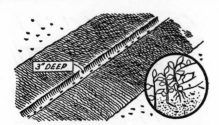

**3.** After the soil has settled, make a drill 3" deep and sow seed 4"-6" apart (a little closer in autumn) and 2" deep. Carefully firm down the soil and water. Soaking of seed overnight prior to sowing helps speed germination, but is not indispensable.

**6.** Water and cultivate weekly during the blooming season if weather is warm and dry. Feed with liquid manure or commercial fertilizer twice a month. Spray for aphis and mildew. Next year select, if possible, another location for your sweet peas.

# ZINNIA

**1.** Zinnias are an almost indispensable part of summer and autumn gardens. Bright, warmth-loving, they belong in the hot, sunny border. They vary from tall, large-flowered to dwarf, diminutive-flowered types in all except blue shades.

**4.** While zinnias do not require as generous treatment as many flowers, they respond well to one or two feedings up to the time of budding. A tablespoon of balanced commercial fertilizer to a plant, carefully worked in and followed by watering, is sufficient.

**2.** Zinnias grow easily and rapidly from seed. Sow in flats from early spring to early summer for succession of bloom. They can also be broadcast in the open ground and later thinned to 12"-18" apart, depending on their type.

**5.** Mildew attacks zinnias, especially in the fall, when days are warm and nights cool. As in the case of rust, it is somewhat controlled by watering from below in the early or middle part of the day. Dust affected plants with Bordeaux mixture or sulphur.

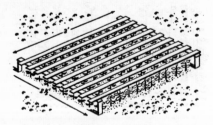

**3.** Plant out zinnias only after danger of frosts is past. Soil that has been manured for a previous crop will not have to be remanured for zinnias. Drainage is important. Shade young plants after planting them out, and water daily until well established.

**6.** Zinnias, like most of the fall-blooming plants, fall prey to various chewing insects, particularly diabroticas. Dust with cryolite, calcium arsenate, or one of the commercial sprays or powders prepared for chewing insects. Select a dry, windless day for spraying or dusting.

# PERENNIALS

The heyday of perennials is at hand.
Modern living calls for less upkeep
and more permanence; hence we offer
a longer list of perennials than annuals. They require study, for their
needs are usually more exacting than
those of annuals, and their propagation more varied. Refer back to the
division on "Garden Techniques"
when dealing with "Perennials," for
their culture involves careful attention to such fundamentals as Soils,
Drainage, Dividing, Cultivation, Staking and Watering.

●

# ANEMONE JAPONICA

**1.** The Japanese Windflower (*Anemone japonica*) is a long lived perennial that blooms from late summer through fall. It is a graceful plant, and grows 4'-5' high. The two best known varieties are Whirlwind, double white, and Queen Charlotte, a double silvery-pink. There are numerous named varieties.

**4.** *Anemone japonica* needs deep, rich soil, afternoon shade and plenty of moisture. Dig deeply and add manure some weeks before planting. If the soil is dry, add peat or leaf-mold, or both, and water well. Wind-flowers like some acidity.

**2.** Windflowers can be propagated by division of the old clumps and by root cuttings. The latter method is the most productive, though the resulting plants will not bloom for 2 years. *Anemone japonica* requires several years to become well established and should not often be disturbed.

**5.** The rooted cuttings, made in fall or spring, can be planted out the following year. When tipping plants out of their pots, take care not to break the ball of soil around the roots. This is best prevented by watering them the day before planting.

**3.** Root cuttings, 1½"-2" long, may be placed horizontally in a flat of seed compost (see Seed Sowing) and covered with ½" of the same mixture. In a few weeks the plants will be ready to pot up. Use an extra part of loam in the potting mixture.

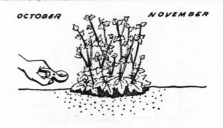

**6.** In the late fall, after flowering, cut the plants to the ground and give a dressing of old manure. Very old plants may need dividing, and spreading clumps restrained. Combine *Anemone japonica* with delphiniums, phlox, lilies, or *Thalictrum dipterocarpum* (Meadow Rue).

# CAMPANULA

**1.** The campanula or bellflower family includes some of the loveliest of all flowers, usually in shades of blue, lavender or white. Perennial bellflowers are propagated by seed sown in spring or summer, by division in spring or fall, or by cuttings.

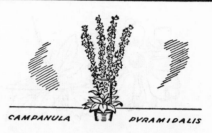

**4.** The stately Chimney Bellflower is unique. Sow seed in spring or fall. Plant toward the back of the shady border, or in large pots or tubs. Stake early to keep heavy spikes from leaning. Feed potted plants liquid manure once weekly before they bloom.

**2.** One of the best-known campanulas is the Canterbury Bell, a biennial. Seed should be started in early summer, grown under fairly cool conditions, and the plants put out in early fall. They will bloom the following year.

**5.** Some of the choicest campanulas are rock garden varieties. Though too numerous to mention, some of the loveliest are *C. carpatica, fragilis, garganica, isophylla alba* and *isophylla,* blue, *rotundifolia* (Bluebells of Scotland), and *C. sarmatica.* Most of these are propagated by cuttings or division.

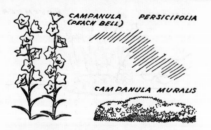

**3.** Campanulas have a wide range of uses. For an attractive, permanent edging in partial shade, no plant can surpass *Campanula muralis. Campanula persicifolia,* the Peach-Leaved Bluebell, is lovely in the perennial border. The variety Telham Beauty is especially choice.

**6.** Most of the rock garden campanulas can also be used for hanging baskets, pots and shady window boxes. *Campanula isophylla alba* is especially suitable. Its starry white flowers often cascade down 2′ and bloom late into the fall.

# CARNATION

**1.** Soil for carnations should be "sweet" and well drained. Lime, crushed plaster, woodash or bonemeal are beneficial. The outdoor carnation flowers in summer and makes its new flowering wood at the same time. Carnations grow easily from seed. Chabaud varieties flower 6 months after sowing.

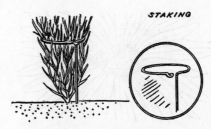

**4.** Carnations usually require staking when in bloom, due to the weight of the flowers on rather weak stems. In large beds planted solidly with carnations, the plants frequently hold each other up and the lack of individual staking is not particularly noticed.

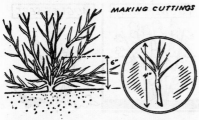

**2.** Make stem cuttings of carnations in spring when new growth has stiffened. Make them not over 4″ long, cutting between the nodes, and insert in sand. When rooted in 4 or 5 weeks, pot up in a mixture of sand, loam and leafmold in equal parts.

**5.** Disbud for large blooms. As with roses, dahlias and other flowers, the side buds are usually removed, leaving one center bud to develop to full size. Feeding with liquid fertilizer before buds begin to color will also increase the size of blooms.

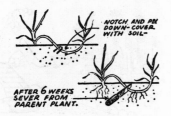

**3.** Outdoor carnations are commonly propagated by layers. Select a lower stem of a strong plant, notch on the underside and peg down the notched section to hold it in place. Cover with soil, mixed with a little sand. Detach when rooted.

**6.** After flowering cut back to 6″-10″ from the ground, cutting to a leaf bud, which will later break out as a new shoot. These will give material for cuttings. Never take more than about 6 cuttings at a time from one plant.

# CHRYSANTHEMUM

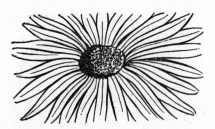

**1.** Chrysanthemums, natives of China and Japan, have been cultivated over 100 years. The first plant was sent from France to Kew Gardens in 1780. Hardy, free-flowering, easily grown, they are available in many types, ranging from the very large to tiny buttons and pompons.

**2.** The usual method of propagating chrysanthemums is by cuttings or division. Make cuttings of young shoots taken in March or April from plants grown the previous year. Make cuttings 4"-5" long and place in flats of sand or in a closed propagating case.

**3.** In 3 or 4 weeks, when the cuttings are rooted, pot them individually in 3" pots. Place the pots in frame which should be kept close and protected from cold and direct sunlight. In a few days, give them more light and air.

**4.** When dividing chrysanthemums, select strong-rooted single pieces from the outside of the clump. Discard the old center. Cut back divisions to 3 or 4 pairs of leaves. Plant 18"-24" apart in ground that has been dug and manured several weeks, or better, months ahead.

**5.** Keep plants cut back until midsummer. Water, but not too generously. In August stop cutting back, increase water and keep cultivated. Remove the first, or crown bud to encourage lateral shoots. Retain the center bud on laterals and disbud the others as seems fit.

**6.** Staking may be necessary, especially for chrysanthemums grown in rows for cutting purposes. Do not allow plants to dry out. Feed once a week between budding and flowering with liquid fertilizer. Watch for aphis, diabroticas, red spider, mildew and rust. Spray regularly.

# COLUMBINE

**1.** Columbines have many advantages. They are easily raised, grow well in shady places, are available in many beautiful shades, and have attractive foliage that is an asset when the plant is not in bloom. Most are border plants, but a few are suitable for rock gardens.

**4.** Columbines will not flower until their second year, but they can be planted out in the autumn following sowing, provided one does not allow them to become overgrown with larger plants or drowned out in heavy rains. They are especially good middle-distance plants.

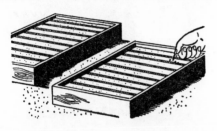

**2.** Columbines are shade lovers and need cool treatment throughout their culture. Sow the seed in May or June, or soon as available. Select a good strain of seed. The quality of columbine is determined by the length of the spurs, the excellence of the colors, and the vigor of growth.

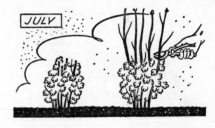

**5.** Plant them with Japanese Windflower, Meadow Rue (*Thalictrum dipterocarpum*), which has similar foliage, lilies, ferns, primroses and campanulas. Cut off seed pods as soon as they appear and remove dead leaves. Columbines are rarely untidy.

**3.** Throughout the warm summer months, the young pricked-out plants must be kept shaded and watered. Cutivate the flats occasionally, for with constant watering, mold or moss may appear.

**6.** Columbines can be divided in autumn. Replant them immediately. Trim cleanly any broken or torn roots and cut back old stems to the base of the plant. Make new sowings every 3 or 4 years to replace old, woody plants. Watch for mealy bug and aphis.

# DELPHINIUM

**1.** The delphinium is often referred to as an aristocrat among flowers. When well grown and properly used it adds a dignity and distinction to the garden that is rarely afforded by other flowers. Watch for new and improved strains that are frequently appearing.

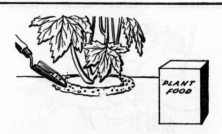

**4.** Delphiniums grow vigorously and flower so heavily that they demand much food in return. Complete commercial fertilizers or cow manure, supplemented with applications of liquid manure during the growing season, are satisfactory. Bonemeal and woodash are also beneficial.

**2.** The usual methods of propagating delphiniums are by seed sown in July or March and planted out 2 months later (in temperate climates); by cutting of young shoots in spring, or by division of large clumps in autumn. The best plants are grown from freshly collected seed.

**5.** In late spring, when new growth has grown to 6″ or 8″, thin out the weaker, crowded shoots, leaving 6 sturdy, well placed shoots. By no means allow plants to form seed, unless you wish to collect it. Well grown delphiniums always give 2 crops of bloom, sometimes three.

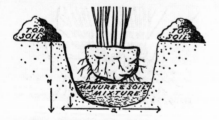

**3.** Delphiniums should be planted with as much care as roses. Lift large clumps with a good ball of earth around the roots. Plant in perfectly drained, previously enriched soil. Keep crowns above the surface and protect young shoots from birds, snails and slugs.

**6.** After plants have bloomed, cut down all stalks to 4″ or 5″. In cold sections, protect the crown with straw or leaves and do not attempt to move until spring. Mildew can best be prevented by planting mildew-resistant strains and by giving them open positions and surface watering. New mildew sprays also help.

# FOXGLOVE

**1.** Foxgloves are one of the few plants that thrive in moist, shaded places and in acid soil. In addition, they are stately and dignified, having spirelike flower spikes. Colors include white, primrose yellow, apricot, rose, pink and cream, and various spotted varieties.

**4.** Foxgloves grow so rapidly that they should not be confined for long in a flat. Plant them out in autumn in their permanent places. By the following spring or early summer they will flower. They combine happily with ferns, columbine, cineraria and lilies.

**2.** Seed sown in early summer will produce plants that will flower the following summer. The foxglove is a biennial and should be grown anew each year. The seed is fine and should be covered very lightly in shallow drills. Keep moist and prick out when 2 sets of leaves have developed.

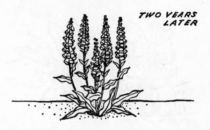

**5.** The soil for foxgloves should be rich with humus and moisture holding, though not poorly drained. Plant them in irregular groups in the background and give them plenty of space. Foxgloves are most effective when planted in drifts of 1 color.

**3.** Young plants should be grown on through the summer in flats in a lathhouse or some shaded place, perhaps under a tree. Keep them sprayed over on warm days. Foxgloves enjoy the same cultural treatment as cinerarias.

**6.** While it is occasionally possible to divide foxgloves, it is better to grow them anew from seed as one would other biennials, such as Canterbury Bells. One sometimes finds older plants growing in particularly suitable locations, but they usually die out after one season.

# GERBERA

**1.** The easiest and most usual method of propagating gerbera is by seed sown in August. However, they can be lifted and divided in spring, preferably between February and April. Lift them with a spading fork so as to avoid cutting roots.

**4.** After the first divisions, make smaller ones with a sharp knife. Take care not to cut through crown buds. A fair-sized gerbera will divide into 4 or 5 pieces.

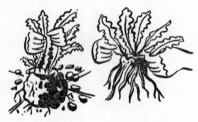

**2.** Shake the soil off the roots. This will enable you to see where the divisions can best be made. If you cannot replant immediately, "heel" in the lifted plants and keep them moist until planting time.

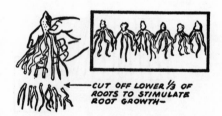

CUT OFF LOWER ⅓ OF ROOTS TO STIMULATE ROOT GROWTH—

**5.** The final divisions are also made with a knife. Each should have 1 or 2 buds. Remove all old, withered leaves. Before planting cut back the roots about ⅓ to balance the tops and roots.

**3.** A 3 or 4-year old gerbera plant frequently measures 1 foot across. The first division is made by pulling the clump apart with one's hands. It will separate into large pieces.

PLANT WITH CROWN PROJECTING—

**6.** Plant divisions with the roots pointing directly downward. The crown must be above the ground level, since gerbera is susceptible to crown rot.

# GYPSOPHILA

**1.** Gypsophila is commonly called Baby's Breath, because of the myriad tiny white or pink flowers that cover the plants and give them the appearance of misty clouds. The annuals are useful for cutting, the perennials for planting in borders.

**4.** Annual gypsophila, available in white and pink, are florists' standbys. *Gypsophila muralis*, *repens*, and *G. cerastioides* are rock garden types. The varieties *paniculata* and *paniculata flore pleno* (double), and *pacifica* are the white, double white, and pink perennial forms.

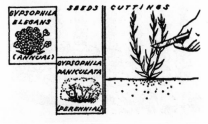

**2.** Both annual and perennial types can be grown from seed, the annual in spring, the perennial in summer or fall. Annual gypsophila can also be sown in the open ground, where it should not be thinned out too much. Perennials may be propagated by basal stem cuttings and by division of large clumps.

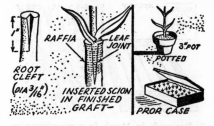

**5.** Bristol Fairy (double white) is propagated by cleft-grafting in fall. Graft strong scions 3"-4" long on roots (pencil size) of *G. paniculata*. Pot up the grafts or place them in a propagating case. Water, shade and keep close until rooted. Plant out in late spring.

**3.** Gypsophila is an excellent foil for spectacular flowers such as Oriental Poppy, flaming phlox, or delphinium. If planted behind earlier-blooming plants, their billowy masses of flowers can be pulled down to cover the bare space. This practice is often called "pegging."

**6.** Cut back perennial gypsophilas after blooming. Mark their positions with stakes, for they leave few traces during winter. In bouquets and flower arrangements, as in the garden, gypsophila adds a light, dainty touch.

# HOLLYHOCK

**1.** Few realize how ancient is the hollyhock—that it was cultivated in China 1000 years before it was introduced into England. It stood beside the gates and front doors of early Colonial homes in America and has since been associated with cottages and fences.

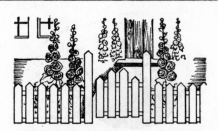

**4.** Hollyhocks grow in ordinary soil and without special care. Plant them 2 feet apart. Use them either for background or for points of accent near entrances or at corners. Their heights usually vary a little, adding to their artistic value.

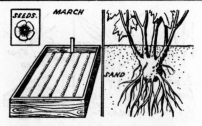

**2.** Sow seeds in March in a greenhouse or frame; in June in the open ground where they are to remain; or in an outdoor seedbed from which they should be transplanted the next spring. You may also propagate them by suckers from the root crown. These suckers result from placing hollyhocks in sand, with the root crown covered.

**5.** Hybridists have produced annual hollyhocks, which means that we can now have them in bloom 6 months after sowing seed. One such hybrid is Indian Spring, a beautiful rose-pink with apricot overtones. Many separate shades in both single and double forms are also available.

**3.** Any tap-rooted plant, such as the hollyhock, is best grown in pots, since the long root can then grow downward with less impediment. In planting, take care that the root points directly downward. Plant a little deeper than it was formerly, for hollyhocks have a tendency to heave upward.

**6.** The only serious disease affecting hollyhock is rust. It is said to winter over on a weed that is a member of the hollyhock family, *Malva rotundifolia*, also known as Cheeses. Eradicate the weed, burn affected plants and weeds, and spray with Bordeaux mixture as a preventive measure.

# ICELAND POPPY

**1.** Iceland poppies are among our brightest winter and spring flowers. They like full sun, perfect drainage and a light soil. New hybrids keep appearing, and gardeners should watch for them. They come in a bewildering array of colors, with the exception of blue, purple and bright red.

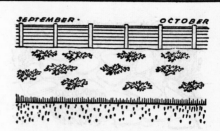

**4.** If possible, plant Iceland poppies in raised beds. Water standing about their roots is the most common cause of failure. If the soil is heavy, add coarse, sandy material to lighten it. Water well after planting, but do not keep them too wet after they are established.

**2.** Sow seed in late summer or early fall, for the best flowers are produced on plants set out while the ground is still warm. Established before cold weather, they will bloom with the frost hoary on their slender stems.

**5.** Solid beds of Iceland poppies—yellow, orange, salmon or white—brighten otherwise colorless winter gardens. They combine well with tulips, and continue to flower after the tulips have faded. Blue, white, yellow or apricot violas make a good edging for beds of Iceland poppies.

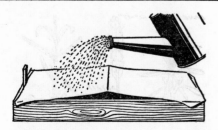

**3.** Take care not to overwater seed boxes, for Iceland poppies damp off easily. If the seed box dries out before germination has taken place (though it should not, for they grow quickly), sprinkle on top of the paper, not the soil. The seed is fine and is easily washed out.

**6.** By June, the main flowering period is over, for Iceland poppies suffer in hot sun, and one must part with them. Their vigorous production seems too much for them and, though perennial, they do not usually live over another year. Their ease of culture, however, makes them quite as useful as any annual.

# LAVENDER

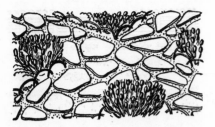

**1.** No sunny garden should be without lavender. It is easily propagated, either from seed sown in fall or spring, or cuttings. Plant them along paths, near gates, in borders, anywhere so long as they have sun; drainage and no manure.

**4.** *Lavandula pedunculata* is most decorative. Its silvery-grey cut leaf is quite different and its flowers are a beautiful lavender-blue. It is a plant choice enough for the perennial border. Lift and pot it up for the winter where cold is extreme, for it is tender.

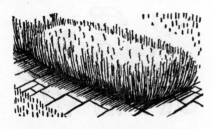

**2.** The English and French lavenders make beautiful low hedges. English lavender is the traditional sachet type, whose flowers are harvested in summer; French lavender blooms all year except in cold climates. Both need renewing every 4 or 5 years.

**5.** English lavender also comes in a dwarf form which makes attractive low hedges and edgings. While lavenders are usually associated with herb gardens, they are by no means to be confined there. A rose garden is never so sweet as when hedged with lavender.

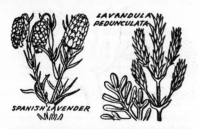

**3.** Spanish lavender (*Lavandula stoechas*) is a small, rounded plant with short flower spikes. It is good between pavings, in herb gardens and in dry borders. *Lavandula pedunculata*, a fairly recent introduction, is the least hardy of lavenders.

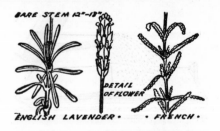

**6.** French lavender (*L. dentata*) differs from English lavender in that it has green, finely dentate leaves, darker lavender flowers, and blooms most of the year. Its foliage is more fragrant than its flowers. It is easily grown from seed and cuttings.

# LUPIN

**1.** One of the horticultural sensations in recent years is the Russell lupin, developed by an English hybridist. This strain is noted for its remarkably vigorous plants, the length of the flower spikes and the range and beauty of rainbow colors in which they are available.

**4.** Perhaps the best method of raising annual lupin is to sow the seed directly in the ground where they are to grow. This can be done in autumn or spring. Careful watering is necessary, before and after germination. Drying out is usually fatal.

**2.** Sow seed in autumn or spring in pots, covering seed to its own depth and soaking the pot from below. Lupin seed is hard coated and should be nicked, or soaked in water to facilitate germination. Before seedlings appear, keep covered with a glass and paper.

PERENNIAL

**5.** The soil for perennial lupin must be rich, moisture holding, but perfectly drained. Work in manure well ahead of planting. Being members of the pea family, they also like limey soil. When well established plants begin to set buds, feed with liquid manure.

**3.** Wipe and turn the glass each day, and remove it when the seedlings appear. Pot up small seedlings when 2 sets of leaves have grown. Move them early, for lupins transplant badly when roots become large.

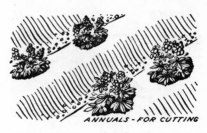

ANNUALS - FOR CUTTING

**6.** Annual lupin, which are usually grown for cutting purposes, are always sown directly in the ground. Prepare the soil well, make drills or furrows 3″ deep and sow as for sweet peas. Thin out to 10″-12″, water generously as they come into flower.

# MICHAELMAS DAISY

**1.** Most of the hybrid Michaelmas daisies are descendants of wild asters of North America, many of which may still be seen along the roadsides, particularly in the eastern part of the United States, and more especially in New England.

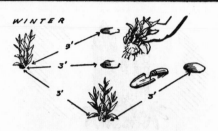

**4.** Due to their habit of spreading so rapidly, hardy asters, as they are also called, should be planted at least 2'-3' apart. Annuals, which can later be removed, may be planted in the spaces that will eventually be filled by the growing plants.

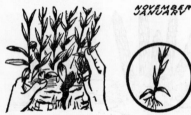

**2.** Yearly division of plants is advisable, for Michaelmas daisies spread astonishingly and will crowd out other plants. Use only small, rooted pieces from the outside of the clump. Many growers prefer making stem cuttings each fall and planting them out in spring.

**5.** As the Michaelmas daisies start growing, thin out to 3 or 4 strong shoots. This will result in a generally healthier plant and a better quality of bloom. At this time also remove any shoots that are crowding nearby plants.

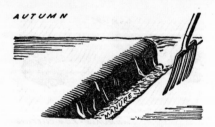

**3.** Rich, moist soil and an open, sunny position are preferred by Michaelmas daisies. Prepare the ground as for other perennials (see Perennial Borders) and allow it to settle before planting. Ample watering while they are coming into flower is also necessary.

**6.** Goldenrod, various sunflowers such as helenium, heliopsis, and helianthus, and rudbeckia are effective planted with Michaelmas daisies. Dwarf Michaelmas daisies are among our best perennials for the front of the border. If they become mildewed in late summer or fall, use one of the new mildew sprays.

# ORIENTAL POPPY

**1.** *Papaver orientale* or Oriental poppy is the answer to the gardener's prayer for a plant with an exciting, exotic character. A dull border planted entirely with plants of quieter tones is given life and interest when splashed with its vivid flaming colors.

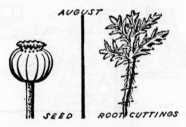

**2.** All poppies are easily grown from seed. The Oriental poppy, however, is best propagated from root cuttings in August, when the plant is most dormant. Proceed as with other root cuttings and cover with light, sandy loam. Keep moist, though not wet, until rooted.

**3.** Oriental poppies, like all poppies, are tap rooted and must not often be disturbed. When rooted, the cuttings should be potted. They can later be transplanted into their permanent places with little or no disturbance to the root system.

**4.** Many of the larger Oriental poppies are heavy headed and lean badly unless staked. If done early, the stake (or stakes) will be concealed by the oncoming growth. Sturdy, erect stems from the start will also result.

**5.** Oriental poppies enjoy good soil and plenty of food and water. After cutting them back in the autumn, give them a dressing of manure, which can be forked under in spring. This will serve as a mulch as well as a feeding.

**6.** Being large, bulky plants, Oriental poppies need much space and can therefore be used only in large borders. They combine well with delphinium, Shasta daisies, gypsophila, and blue flax. Keep seed pods removed.

# PELARGONIUM

**1.** The showiest members of the Pelargonium or Geranium family are the Martha Washington geraniums. Their large flowers and attractive foliage make them especially desirable as pot plants. They are not quite as hardy as the ordinary geranium (zonal pelargonium).

**4.** In fall, when the main flowering period is past, pelargoniums can be pruned back to within about 4″ of the base. Pelargoniums growing outside must not be pruned until spring. Neither should they be heavily watered or fed.

**2.** The best pelargoniums are grown from cuttings taken between August and October. Make cuttings 3″-4″ long, place in sand in a flat or propagating case, and keep moist and shaded until they root. Pot up when well rooted and place in a coldframe.

**5.** Martha Washington geraniums enjoy partial shade except in cool climates along the seacoast, where they thrive in full sun. Zonal pelargoniums (common geraniums) want full sun, as do the scented geraniums. Ivy geraniums, which make excellent ground covers and window box material, like part shade.

**3.** When the potted cuttings have grown to 6″ or 7″, pinch out the tips to encourage side shoots. Less vegetative growth means more flowers. In summer, with buds starting, plants can be fed with liquid manure or with a teaspoon of commercial fertilizer to each pot, watered in.

**6.** In addition to their usefulness for potwork and massed planting, pelargoniums, particularly the Martha Washingtons, make effective cut flowers. Hybridists are developing better and wider ranges of color.

# PENTSTEMON

**1.** The pentstemon, or Beardtongue, is a perennial which has not always been used to its fullest advantage. Too often one finds it poorly grown and in unattractive colors. It is now available in beautiful, clear colors, in both tall and dwarf forms.

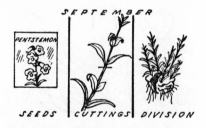

*SEPTEMBER*

*SEEDS* | *CUTTINGS* | *DIVISION*

**2.** Propagate pentstemons from seed, cuttings, division and layers. Sow seed in fall in temperate climates, in spring in cold climates. Vegetative propagation (cuttings, etc.) ensures exact reproduction of the type, and is very easy. Make cuttings in fall or spring.

*SPRING*

**3.** In all except temperate zones, it is best to wait until spring to plant out pentstemons. In most sections of the Pacific Coast, it is safe to plant them in fall, though a light mulch about their roots is advisable. Plant in sun or light shade.

**4.** As bedding plants pentstemons hardly have an equal. Plant them in masses in front of shrubbery, along drives and fences. Especially fine varieties are the large white, Apple Blossom Pink, Scarlet and Crimson Bedder. These varieties come true from cuttings, layers and division.

**5.** In temperate regions, cut back pentstemons in fall, after the main flowering season is past. They will send out new growth, from which cuttings may be made. Wait until spring where winters are severe. Pentstemons are best renewed every 3 or 4 years.

**6.** Among the less known pentstemons are some dwarf, compact, rock garden types which will also serve nicely as edgings or low border plants. One of the choicest is *Pentstemon heterophyllus* Blue Bedder, a California native. It is heat-loving and easy to grow.

# PEONY

**1.** The peony is an ancient Chinese plant which is beloved in both Chinese and Japanese gardens. It has been cultivated in Europe since 1800, and shortly after in America. There are two types grown, the herbaceous peony, which grows 2'-3' high, and the Tree Peony, which grows to 6'.

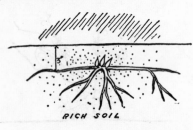

RICH SOIL

**2.** The usual method of propagation is by division of the roots with a crown bud attached. Plant 2" or 3" below the surface in deeply dug soil in which manure has been turned under at least 18". Plant in fall. Light shade is preferable, though tree roots are to be avoided.

**3.** Layering of procumbent stems in the fall is also possible. Proceed in the usual way (see Layering) and weight down the layered stem with a brick or rock. The rooted stem can be severed from the parent plant the following autumn.

SPRING

BONE MEAL

**4.** It is the initial enrichment of the soil that is really important, but an autumn dressing of manure or steamed bonemeal is also good. Gently stir in the bonemeal around the plant, taking care not to disturb near-surface roots.

**5.** During the flowering period, keep faded blooms cut. Plants that receive morning sun and afternoon shade will have fresher, longer-lasting flowers than those in full sun. When entering dormancy in autumn, peonies should be cut to the ground.

**6.** The Tree Peony has tall, woody stems which assume interesting, "Japanesque" outlines. Its flowers are usually white or pink. This type is pruned only lightly. Peonies make beautiful cut flowers, but must be arranged with much taste to be really effective.

# PHLOX PANICULATA

**1.** Western gardeners need not look longingly at the magnificent phlox in Eastern gardens. It will not be possible to succeed in hotter, drier sections of the West, but certainly phlox can be raised to near-perfection in the Northwest and in moister, coastal sections of California.

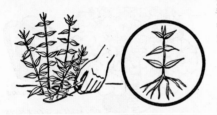

**2.** The common method of propagating perennial phlox is by cuttings of the young growth in autumn or spring, or by rooted divisions of the old clump. Grow cuttings in sandy compost until rooted. Use only strong divisions from the outside of the clump when dividing old plants.

**3.** Phlox are food and water-loving. Soil must be rich and retentive of moisture. Avoid fresh manure around young plants, but work in plenty farther down. Light shade is preferable where summers are warm and rainless. Water heavily around roots to counteract atmospheric dryness.

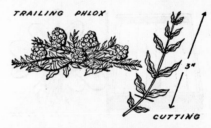

**4.** In winter or early spring, mulch perennial phlox with well rotted manure. This will serve as a covering for surface roots that may have become washed by heavy rains, while the food in the manure will leach down to the feeding roots. Thin out crowded shoots in spring.

*TRAILING PHLOX*

*3"*

*CUTTING*

**5.** There are several perennial creeping, or prostrate phloxes suitable for edgings, bulb coverings, rock gardens and rock walls. Most of them have rooted stems which can be removed from the plant. They can also be grown from cuttings (2"-3" long) in spring and started in sand.

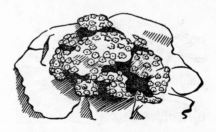

**6.** Among the loveliest of the dwarf phlox are *Phlox subulata* in white, pink and blue, *P. amoena* (pink), *P. arendsi* (lavender), *P. divaricata canadensis* (native of the eastern U. S. and a lovely lavender-blue), and *Phlox ovata* (rosy red). All but *P. divaricata* like sun.

# PRIMROSE

**1.** Until a few years ago, the Cowslip *(Primula veris)* English primrose *(P. vulgaris)* and the mixed hybrids *(P. polyantha)* were the only hardy species widely grown. Plant collectors, working mainly in China, have lengthened this list, until it now includes numerous types and colors, and covers a long season.

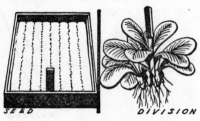

SEED        DIVISION

**2.** Sow seed in spring or fall in a mixture of light loam, leafmold and sand in equal parts. Gently press (not cover) the fine seed into the soil surface. Water from below and cover with glass and paper. Divide primroses in late summer or early fall.

**3.** Prick out seedlings when large enough to handle. Use the same soil mixture with ½ part screened peat added. Some growers prefer to handle tiny plants with a small pronged stick. By autumn the plants can be set out in a shady or partly shady spot.

**4.** Primroses are a delightful accompaniment to spring bulbs, especially narcissi. They are particularly effective when naturalized together in drifts, the primroses forming a carpet for the higher, graceful-stemmed daffodils or other narcissi.

LIQUID MANURE

PRIMULA SINENSIS

**5.** There are primulas, called florists' types, which make good pot plants. Among these are *P. obconica* and *P. sinensis stellata.* Start both very early in spring to flower at Christmas. Treat seed and seedlings in same manner as ordinary primroses. Feed with liquid manure when coming into flower.

**6.** Unlike the regular primroses, such as *P. veris,* the florists' types do not ordinarily last over from 1 year to the next. They are treated as annuals, and fresh seed is sown each year.

# SALVIA

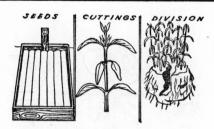

**1.** There are perennial and annual types of salvia, both of which are among our most useful summer and fall-blooming plants. Perennials are propagated by the 3 methods illustrated. Those grown from seed will, with the exception of one, *Salvia farinacea,* take 2 years to bloom.

**4.** *Salvia farinacea* is good combined with *Phlox drummondi,* pink, cream, yellow or white zinnias, pale yellow marigolds, pentstemons, particularly the pink or white, and ageratum. Its soft, misty color and spikey form make it a good mixer.

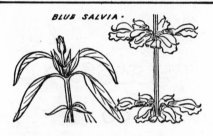

**2.** *Salvia farinacea* deserves special mention as a plant that combines beautifully with other perennials and annuals and blooms until hard frosts. The varieties Blue Bedder and the more recent Royal Blue both have tall lavender-blue spikes that stand 3'-4' high.

**5.** There are several perennial forms which belong in the perennial border. Among them are *Salvia azurea grandiflora,* large flowered and pale sky-blue; *Salvia pitcheri,* a deeper periwinkle-blue, and *Salvia uliginosa,* bright sky-blue, and a rampant grower which must be watched. All grow to 4' or 5'.

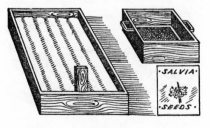

**3.** The annual red salvia grows easily from seed and is an old favorite with some gardeners. The color is a bit difficult and one should use it carefully and, if possible, by itself. *Salvia farinacea* grows almost as quickly from seed and can be treated as an annual

**6.** After flowering, cut back the perennial forms and discard the annual form. It will be found advisable to divide the perennials every 3 or 4 years. They like rich soil and moisture during their flowering period.

# VIOLETS

**1.** The violet (*Viola odorata*) is a close relative of the viola or Tufted Pansy. While the viola is propagated by seed and sometimes by cuttings, the true violet is inceased by divisions of the crown or by offsets and runners.

**4.** Plant offshoots or runners in winter, 1' apart, firming in roots and watering thoroughly. Plant in shade or in a position receiving morning sun and afternoon shade. Generous watering helps to prevent attacks from red spiders, which work best under dry conditions.

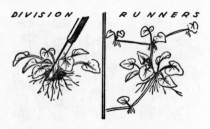

**2.** Division of the crown is often unsatisfactory, because of the woodiness of the old crowns. The creeping stems of violets root at the joints; sections of these roots, if replanted, will form new plants. Young offshoots can be taken after the plants have bloomed and rooted in flats of sand.

**5.** Lift and divide violets every 2 years in spring, in order that they may be well established by fall, at which time violets often begin to bloom. It is best to divide in fall in hot climates, although slightly retarded bloom may result.

**3.** Violets respond to generous soil conditions, but will grow in ordinary soil if not too heavy. Enrichment with well decayed manure, occasional additions of lime or gypsum (every 3 or 4 years) and remaking of beds when they become overgrown are worthwhile.

**6.** Violets frequently bloom shyly for a number of reasons, among which may be overcrowding, poor stock, unsuitable location, or impoverished soil. If the latter reason be the cause, a top dressing of compost mixed with commercial fertilizer, applied in fall, helps produce bloom.

# BULBS

Bulbs play an increasingly important part in Western gardens, for many of them thrive and increase with little care, are suited to our climatic conditions and can be used in a number of ways. This is particularly true of the South African bulbs which seem so well suited to California conditions, as well as of some of the European and Asiatic species which are adapted to Northwestern conditions. See "Garden Techniques" for general data on bulbs.

# AMARYLLIS

**1.** The Belladonna Lily, or *Amaryllis bella-donna*, is the old favorite which raises large pink fragrant trumpet-shaped flowers on bare stems during the summer. It can be grown outdoors in sheltered positions, and need not be lifted in winter except in severely cold climates.

**4.** Rich compost composed of equal parts of good loam and rotted manure, with a little sand and bonemeal added, is necessary. In late spring or early summer, when buds are forming, feed with liquid manure or with commercial fertilizer, thoroughly watered in.

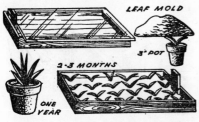

**2.** Hippeastrums are trumpet-shaped flowers which come in reds and white, frequently in striped forms. Their leaves are broad and strap shaped. Seed sown in spring often produces blooming bulbs in 2 years. Pot on from smaller to larger pots as required. Six-inch pots are needed at the 1-year stage.

**5.** It is important to rest hippeastrum after flowering. During this time they are storing up energy for next year's bloom. Plunge them in a frame or in the ground in a position where they receive light shade and little water. Dry them out in winter.

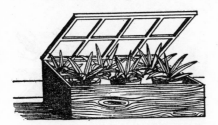

**3.** Hippeastrum are grown on actively through their first winter in a cool greenhouse or frame. During the second winter they are rested. In late winter or early spring they are ready to be forced into growth.

**6.** Hippeastrum are not often grown in the open ground. In any case, they must be brought into the greenhouse for the winter. The amaryllis (*Amaryllis belladonna*) often planted outside, should have a deep, rich, well-drained soil. Water and feed it when it comes into flower.

# ANEMONE AND RANUNCULUS

**1.** Anemone and ranunculus are frequently confused, due to the similarity of foliage and flower. Anemones, however, come in blue and purple shades, whereas ranunculi are always in yellow, orange and red shades, and have longer stems, besides. Both are spring bulbs.

**2.** Both anemone and ranunculus can be grown from seed sown in March. Seed of anemone is fine and light, and must be sown evenly. Both should be grown in flats through their first summer. In winter, keep dry and dormant, and plant out after frosts the next spring.

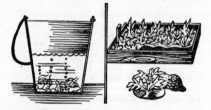

**3.** Before planting, soak bulbs in water for 15 to 20 minutes. Good bulbs will swell; unsuitable bulbs will remain withered looking. Grow them on in flats and plant them out when 5" to 6" high.

**4.** The most serious spring pests are birds, small animals, snails and slugs. Poisoned bait will control snails and slugs. Birds and rabbits (the latter in suburban and country gardens) can be stopped only by wire coverings.

**5.** Spring bulbs and annuals often respond well to pre-flowering feedings of quick fertilizers. Chemical fertilizers, such as sulphate of ammonia, nitrate of soda, or ammonium phosphate, if applied in mild solution (1 teaspoon to 1 gallon of water), frequently help to speed up lagging plants.

**6.** Lift the tubers after the tops have yellowed. Sun-cure them for a few days, then clean and store them in a cool, dry, frost-free place, in flats of clean, dry sand or peat. Keep them out of reach of rodents.

# BEGONIA, TUBEROUS

**1.** Sow seed between January and March as follows: Place 2″ gravel in a flat or shallow pot, then about 1″ fairly coarse compost (⅔ leafmold, ⅓ peat), and add a thin, finely sieved layer of the same mixture on top. Soak the flat or pot from below, then sow seed.

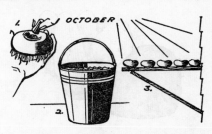

**4.** As foliage begins to wither and yellow in fall, gradually withhold water. When foliage is completely gone, lift the tubers, clean thoroughly, taking care to remove completely old stems. Wash, sun-dry for 24-36 hours, and store in flats of peat in a cool, dry place.

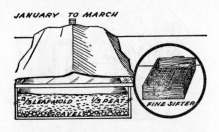

**2.** Cover with glass and paper, lifting and wiping daily until after germination. To maintain the necessary 65°-75° night temperature, artificial heat is required. Prick out 1″ apart at the 3-leaf stage. Continue to transplant as they grow, spacing farther apart or placing in small pots.

**5.** In January or February bring the flats of tubers into a warm place and sprinkle occasionally to cause sprouting. As sprouts appear, place tubers 3″ apart in flats of peat. By March or April tubers will be ready to plant out in the open or pot up.

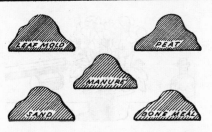

**3.** Well ahead of planting, prepare outdoor beds, adding well rotted manure and lightening with leafmold, peat and sand. Also add a sprinkling of bonemeal. Plant in shade from March to June. Water with gentle overhead sprinklings.

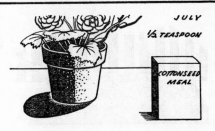

**6.** Pot in 2 parts leafmold and 1 part loam, providing perfect drainage. As the plants bud, feed once or twice with cottonseed meal (½ teaspoon to a plant), or special commercial fertilizers, placed around the rim of the pot or 6″ away from the stem.

# CYCLAMEN

**1.** The Persian cyclamen, found in florists' shops, is one of the most satisfying winter plants. It is not difficult to grow if one understands its needs. Cyclamen can be had in flower 15 months from seed, and are excellent pot plants for cold sections where outdoor growing is not possible.

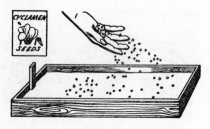

**2.** As soon as fresh seed is obtainable, in May or June, sow in a leafy compost. Germination is slow; usually about 2 months is required, because a small bulb or corm forms beneath the surface before any leaves appear. Prick out after 2 leaves have developed.

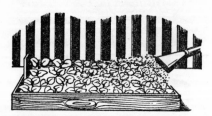

**3.** Prick out and grow young plants through the summer in flats or small pots. Sprinkle lightly on hot days. Established plants which have bloomed need a little moisture in summer, also. Plunging in the ground in a partly shaded place is a safe way to carry them over.

**4.** In warmer parts of the West, cyclamen can safely be planted in the open ground. They bloom in winter with the daphne and Christmas Rose. A planting of pink and white cyclamen beneath a Weeping Cherry is a joy to see. They need morning sun and afternoon shade.

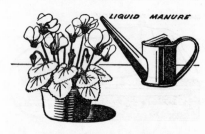

**5.** Pot corms in a mixture of 2 parts loam, 1 part leafmold, 1 part sand, ½ part well decayed manure, and about 1 tablespoon bonemeal to a 5″ or 6″ pot. Cyclamen like being slightly pot bound. Plant with corm slightly raised above the surface. Feed once or twice during growing season.

**6.** Cyclamen are frequently attacked by a small mite which causes growth to become deformed and marred by dark streaks. Spray with a rotenone or nicotine solution. Commercial growers use methyl-bromide with great success.

# DAFFODIL

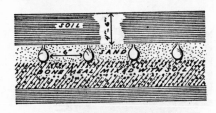

**1.** The daffodil probably holds first place among bulbs that are easy to grow, long lived, gopher proof and excellent cutflowers. Botanically, the daffodil is the trumpet narcissus. It has been crossed and recrossed by hybridizers until it may now be had in an almost infinite variety.

**2.** Plant from early to late fall in deeply dug soil without manure. Bulbs should be covered 2½ times their depth, or about 6″ deep. Add bonemeal to the ground and plant bulbs in a cushion of sand to ensure good drainage.

**3.** Daffodils are ideal for naturalizing (planting in a natural or informal manner). Where many bulbs are to be planted, throw handfuls on the ground and plant them where they fall, observing the above rules. Ground covers can later be sown on top of them.

**4.** Never cut foliage of daffodils or other bulbs while it is green. This deprives the bulb of valuable food material to store away for next year's growth. Instead, fold over the foliage, secure it firmly with a rubber band, and allow it to dry. Summer-blooming plants can be put out between the daffodils.

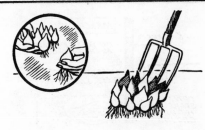

**5.** Daffodils should be lifted and divided every 3 or 4 years to maintain size and quality of bloom. Mosaic, a virus disease which causes a mottled, distorted condition of the leaves, sometimes attacks daffodils. The only control is to lift and burn the bulbs.

**6.** Daffodils and other narcissi can be forced by growing them in bowls or saucers of pebbles and water. This is most often practiced with the Chinese lilies and paper white narcissi, but certain trumpet narcissi will also succeed, especially when started late in autumn.

# DAHLIA

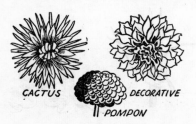

CACTUS  DECORATIVE  POMPON

**1.** Dahlias belong, along with chrysanthemums and zinnias, among the standbys giving autumn color in the garden. To be completely effective in the garden they must be placed with consideration given to texture and to foreground planting. Their greatest use is as cut flowers.

AUGUST-SEPTEMBER

REMOVE SIDE BUDS

**4.** Where quantity of bloom is desired for a landscape effect, little disbudding is done. Where large, specimen flowers are wanted, the center, or crown bud on each shoot is retained and the rest (laterals) are pinched off. Two or 3 sets of leaves below the bud can also be removed.

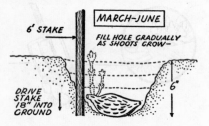

MARCH-JUNE

6' STAKE  FILL HOLE GRADUALLY AS SHOOTS GROW—

DRIVE STAKE 18" INTO GROUND  6"

**2.** Plant after frosts in a sunny open position. They grow best in deep, well drained, not-too-heavy loam. While well rotted manure can be used if applied several months ahead, bonemeal is recommended as the best fertilizer for dahlias. Plant tubers as indicated in the diagram.

FERTILIZER  PHOSPHATES & POTASH

**5.** Dahlias react favorably to surface feedings, especially those supplying phosphorus and potash. Bonemeal, muriate of potash and sulphate of potash supply these elements. Apply in moderate quantity (2 lbs. of bonemeal will supply 10 plants), work in 6" away from the stem, and water.

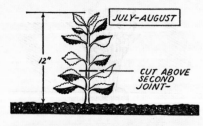

JULY-AUGUST

12"  CUT ABOVE SECOND JOINT—

**3.** Thin out the plant to 3 strong shoots. When these shoots are 12" high, pinch them back to the second pair of leaves. This produces a bushier plant and retards flowering, desirable where late color or succession of bloom is desired.

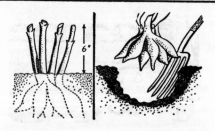

6"

**6.** Several good soakings are necessary during the growing season. After frosts, or when the tops have yellowed, cut back stems to 6" from the ground and lift the tubers. Store in a cool basement or shed in sand or sawdust.

# DAYLILY

**1.** The daylily (Hemerocallis) is so called because its individual flowers last well but 1 day. However, they follow one another so rapidly that the plant hardly ever seems out of bloom. It is one of the finest herbaceous, or perennial, plants.

**4.** Daylilies have a particular value in the perennial border, where plants with long seasons of bloom, hardy characteristics, and few cultural needs are appreciated. Plant them in groups of 3 or more toward the middle of the large border.

LATE FALL OR EARLY SPRING

**2.** Propagation is by division practiced in fall or early spring. Each division should have a crown bud and several strong roots. In replanting, trim back any over-long or broken roots. Dividing is usually not necessary oftener than every 4 or 5 years.

**5.** To prove their versatility, daylilies thrive at pools' edges and near streams, where they can enjoy cool root-runs and warmth above. They should be used only in an informal manner, because of their loose habit of growth and rather untidy foliage.

**3.** For the best effects in the garden, daylilies should be kept clear of faded buds. This will also help to lengthen their period of bloom. In fall, when the main flowering is over, cut back all stems to the ground and clear away all dead foliage.

**6.** They can also be used in rock gardens and on sunny slopes, provided thorough waterings are occasionally given through the summer. Gardeners should watch for new hybrids, especially soft lemon and golden yellows. They are also available in orange and tawny shades.

# GLADIOLUS

**1.** The ancestors of the modern gladioli were favorites of the ancient Greeks and Romans. Easy culture, long season, a wide color range, and longevity give them a first place among summer-flowering bulbs. They are quite inexpensive, are decorative, and almost disease-free.

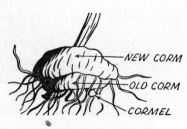

NEW CORM
OLD CORM
CORMEL

**2.** It is possible to grow gladioli from spring-sown seed. These seedlings will produce flowering corms the second or third year. Cormlets, or the tiny corms surrounding the large bulb, can be grown to flowering size in the same manner as seed.

EARLY SPRING

BONE MEAL WORKED INTO SOIL

**3.** Plant full-sized corms 3"-6" deep, depending on the size of the corm. Bonemeal is a safe fertilizer. Manure is possible if it is worked in the autumn previous to planting. In heavy soil, it is well to plant gladioli in cushions of sand. Begin planting in spring as soon as weather permits.

PLANT FOOD

**4.** By planting at 2-week intervals, one can have gladioli in bloom for at least 3 months. As they begin to mature, keep them thoroughly watered and cultivated. Feed with sprinklings of balanced commercial fertilizer once or twice during the growing season.

**5.** The most serious enemy of the gladiolus is thrips. These insects live over on the corms in the winter and are best controlled then. However, if they appear on the plants, use a contact spray containing nicotine, pyrethrum or rotenone, or tartar emetic, available in drugstores.

ALENE LAKES

NAPHTHALENE FLAKES

SOAKING IN CORROSIVE SUBLIMATE-

PAPER BAG

**6.** When the leaves and stalks of gladioli turn brown, lift and dry them in the sun for a few days. Later it will be possible to remove the stalks. The corms should then be stored in a cool, dry place in paper bags in which have been sprinkled naphthalene flakes (a handful to a bag). Remove naphthalene after 2 weeks.

# GLOXINIA

1. The gloxinia is a native of humid, tropical forests whose conditions must be duplicated as closely as possible by those who would successfully grow this unusual bulbous plant. Select high-grade seed; they may be had in blue, purple, pink and crimson shades, and white.

4. Pot the rooted tubers in a mixture of 2 parts leafmold, 1 part peat, and 1 part loam. The pots should be just large enough to accommodate the bulbs. In waterings, remove the sprinkler from the can. Never water gloxinias on their leaves.

2. Gloxinias must be grown in greenhouses or indoors. Sow seed as for tuberous begonias in early February. Cover with glass and keep well shaded during germination, seedling and growing stages, when a temperature of 70°-80° is required.

5. In late summer, the gloxinia will be ready to enter a rest period corresponding to that prevalent in its native habitat. Withhold water, allow leaves to ripen off, and store pots in a cool spot for the winter. Give a little water now and then to keep tubers alive.

3. Gloxinias are also propagated by leaf cuttings, made of mature leaves with a short piece of petiole (stem) attached. These are taken in mid-February and inserted in sand, which must not be kept too wet. Rooting is rapid and small tubers will form.

6. In February, when new growth begins to appear, shake off the old potting soil. Repot in fresh compost (same as above), and keep on the dry side until roots really take hold. Pot on as plants need it, increase watering. Gloxinias begin flowering about June.

# HYACINTH

**1.** Several types of hyacinths are listed in catalogs. The difference in these types, however, is mainly in the size of the bulbs and in the size and number of flowers. In order of size they are: Large Dutch or Common, Miniature Dutch and Roman.

**2.** Sow seed for new varieties. Stock is usually increased by slashing or hollowing out the bottom of the bulb, allowing it to callous for 2-3 weeks, and planting it out in October. By the following June the old bulb will have withered away and in its place will be many small bulblets.

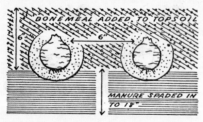

**3.** Soil for hyacinths must be well drained. Well rotted manure, spaded in low, is recommended if the beds have been steadily used. To ensure consistent flowering, plant bulbs at a uniform depth, about 6". Space 6" apart and provide a cushion of sand. Add bonemeal to the top soil.

**4.** Pot hyacinths in September for January bloom. Make a compost of 3 parts loam, 1 part leafmold, 1 part rotted manure, and a little sand. Set the bulb so that its top is just above the surface of the soil. Use one bulb to a 4" or 5" pot, or three to a 7" or 8" pot.

**5.** After watering, place pots in a dark place and cover them with wood shavings, peat, ashes or any material that will keep out light, but not air. When roots are formed (6 weeks for small bulbs, 8 weeks for large), bring pots into light and warmth.

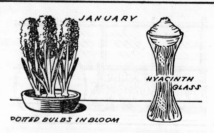

**6.** Avoid watering hyacinths in the hearts of the leaves, for it causes rotting of the flowering stem and eventually of the bulb itself. If flowers tend to bloom low, place forcing caps over pots to draw them up. Hyacinth glasses provide an easy method of growing bulbs.

# IRIS, BEARDED

GERMAN

**1.** Iris fall into two large classes, bearded and beardless. Among the bearded iris, the most important is *Iris germanica*, or the German iris. Most iris are natives of the Mediterranean region and particularly suited to California conditions.

JAPANESE

**4.** The most important members of the second, or beardless, class are Japanese Iris (*Iris kaempferi*). It is possible to grow them quite easily from seed, a good method if one wishes to fill a large space, without any particular attention to color and flower size.

**2.** German iris like a loamy, well drained, medium rich soil. Add lime or woodash to a heavy soil, bonemeal to a light, poor soil. Give them a sunny, open position and divide when crowded, or every 2 or 3 years. If time doesn't permit lifting old clumps, cut out the center with a spade and refill with soil.

**5.** Japanese iris have smaller rhizomes than the German iris and form thick clumps which are difficult to divide without the aid of a knife or sharp spade. Replant divisions without delay, since the roots dry out quickly. They want rich, moist, slightly acid soil.

LIME
OLD PLASTER
OR BONE MEAL

**3.** Rhizomes should be exposed to the sun. Water well after planting in summer or early fall, and then give little or no water. Top dressings of old plaster, lime or bonemeal on established iris beds every 3 or 4 years keep the soil sweet and mellow.

**6.** These iris enjoy wet feet, especially when coming into active growth. The shallow, sunny end of an informal pool is an ideal spot. If the pool is concrete lined, plant tubers in tubs, boxes or pots. The water should just reach the top edge or rim of the containers.

# IRIS - DUTCH, SPANISH, AND ENGLISH

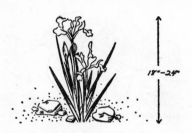

**1.** An increasing number of gardeners are beginning to appreciate the value of bulbous iris, both for cutting and as border flowers. They belong to a group called the Xiphium, and bloom in May and June in the order listed above.

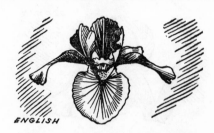

ENGLISH

**4.** English iris, on the other hand, want moist, cool, partially shaded positions. This point should not be hard to remember if one associates them with the fog-cooled British Isles. Give them a deep, leafy, though well drained soil. Plant in August or September.

DUTCH

**2.** The Dutch iris are hybrids of the Spanish type. They have longer, heavier stems and bloom earlier (April-May). Their color range is extensive and includes beautiful shades of blue and purple, yellow, orange, and white. Plant at the same time as tulips.

**5.** This group of bulbous iris should be planted 3″ deep, or twice the depth of the bulb. Place them on a cushion of sand and keep away from fresh manure. Aside from the English iris, they do not want to be under trees. An open position is best.

SPANISH

**3.** The Spanish iris, true to its name and Mediterranean heritage (though it was developed by Dutch growers), loves a warm, sunny, well drained spot. The colors are predominantly yellows, browns, blue and white tones. Bulbs should ripen well in summer.

**6.** Graceful, delicately formed and beautifully shaded flowers on straight stems make iris particularly useful in the perennial or annual spring border. Their period of bloom follows closely upon that of tulips. Suitable ground covers are dwarf nemesia, Virginian stock, and forget-me-nots.

# LILY

**1.** Lilies are quite easily grown from freshly picked seed. Sow the seed in flats, seed pans (shallow pots), or frames, in a soil mixture of 1 part loam, 1 part leafmold, and 1 part sharp sand. Give lilies a cool culture.

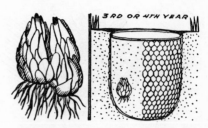

**4.** Lilies can also be propagated from scales, removed from large bulbs and rooted in sand, and, in certain species, from little bulbs (bulbils) growing in axils of the leaves. Protect from gophers by planting bulbs in large wire baskets.

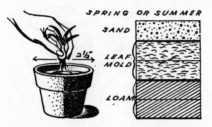

**2.** If sown in a frame, the seed should be placed 1″ apart so that seedlings will not have to be moved until the second year. When the bulbs are about ¼″ long, transplant into 2½″ pots, adding an extra part of leafmold and loam to the compost.

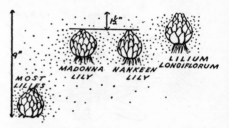

**5.** The planting depth for lily bulbs varies. Generally, plant them 3 times the depth of the bulb. Provide a cushion of sand to improve drainage and help prevent bacterial disease. Bulbs should not remain long out of the ground. Dust with sulphur before planting. Mulch with leaves in winter.

**3.** By the end of the second summer, the little bulbs will be ready to plant out in their permanent beds in a shaded location, where the soil is deep, leafy, moist, and perfectly drained. Many lilies bloom the second or third summers after sowing.

**6.** The regal, stately form of lilies is proverbial. Delphiniums and Madonna lilies are especially lovely together. The Regal Lily is beautiful in solid masses in a fairly sunny location, as is also *L. formosanum*, which flowers in 9 months from seed.

# SOUTH AFRICAN BULBS

FREESIA

**1.** Freesias are very successful in regions where conditions closely approximate those in South Africa. Plant as soon as available in light, rich soil in a sunny position. They bloom 1 year from seed. Divide about every 3 or 4 years. Pot up in cold climates

ORNITHOGALUM

**4.** Also from Africa and the Mediterranean region is the ornithogalum. Though choice varieties exist, the best known species is *O. umbellatum*, commonly called Star-of-Bethlehem, which is apt to become objectionable because of its prolificacy. Culture is similar to freesias.

IXIA

**2.** Ixias are brilliantly colored flowers somewhat resembling miniature gladioli. They are not completely hardy except in temperate climates. Their culture is the same as that for freesias. Plant 1″ deep, 3″-4″ apart, or grow in pots. They are quite easily grown from seed.

MORAEA

**5.** Similar to iris are the moraeas, natives, for the most part of warm, sunny African plains. One of the hardiest and most widely grown is *Moraea glaucopis* (also called Pavonia), or Peacock Iris. There are at least 65 species, many of which are hardy in all but the coldest climates.

SPARAXIS

**3.** Sparaxis are closely related to ixias. They are lower in height (6″-12″) and have larger individual flowers in red, yellow, purple and white shades. Plant in fall or early spring in a sunny, perfectly drained position. As cut flowers they are effective and last well.

SCHIZOSTYLIS

**6.** The corms of the Kaffir Lily (*Schizostylis*) are planted out in late spring and bloom in fall. The best variety for outdoor culture is the variety Mrs. Hegarty, which has rose-pink flowers. The crimson-flowered *S. coccinea* blooms very late and is better for pot culture in all except mild climates.

# TULIPS-in Pots

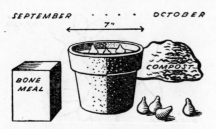

**1.** Use only early-flowering tulips for forcing in pots. Potted up in September or October, they bloom in January or February. Place 3 bulbs in a 7″ or 8″ pot. Cover twice their depth. One of the best early tulips for pot work is Fantasy. a Parrot type.

**4.** Tulips are food-loving, but should never come directly into contact with manure. For this reason, manure is never included in their potting compost; bonemeal, a safe fertilizer, is added instead. Supplementary feedings during active growth are beneficial.

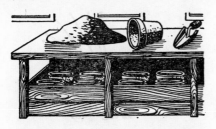

**2.** During the next 6-8 weeks, treat them as you would hyacinths, that is, keep them in a cool, dark place until roots have formed. It should not be necessary to water the pots between potting and removing them from the dark.

**5.** After being brought into the greenhouse, conservatory or house from the forcing pit, tulips should be given plenty of light and warmth. As with hyacinths, do not water into the center of the leaves. Stand pots on gravel to provide circulation and improve drainage.

**3.** It is not infrequent for tulips to bloom low, both in pots and in the garden. An application of quick fertilizer in solution often helps to bring their stems up. If this does not prove a success, try a forcing cap with a hole at the top.

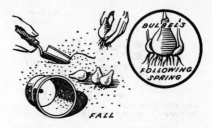

**6.** Tulips cannot be successfully forced in pots for 2 consecutive years. Any forcing greatly depletes and exhausts bulbs. Therefore, tulips, as well as many other potted bulbs, including narcissi, should be planted out in the open ground the following season.

# VARIOUS BULBS

**1.** The *Fritillaria imperialis* (Crown Imperial) is an effective bulbous plant with flowers in shades of yellow, orange and red. Plant 6" deep in rich, moist, leafy soil, and shade from midday sun. Give bulbs plenty of room and lift and replant every third year. They make good tub and pot plants.

**4.** *Milla biflora* comes from Mexico and has the common name Estrellitas (Little Stars), because of its starlike white flowers. Their outside culture in mild climates is the same as for gladioli. Or grow in pots, using the same mixture as for hyacinths. Keep fairly cool. They bloom in 3 months.

**2.** Lachenalias (Cape Cowslips) can be grown outdoors in mild regions, and in pots elsewhere. Use 5 or 6 bulbs for a 6" pot. Use a soil mixture of 2 parts light loam and 1 part leafmold. Plant in a cushion of sand. Keep cool and a little dry until roots form. Then give light, warmth and moisture.

**5.** The brilliant red flowers of *Lycoris radiata* appear in the fall, while the foliage comes in March, then disappears. The flowers resemble *Nerine sarniensis*. Pot in early fall to bloom at Christmas. If grown outdoors in any except mild climates, they should be lifted in autumn.

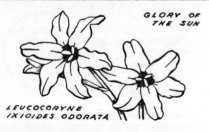

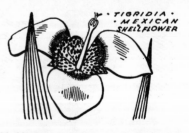

**3.** No list of bulbs is complete without *Leucocoryne ixioides*, or the Glory-of-the-Sun, whose exquisitely fragrant, lavender-blue, slender-stemmed flowers bloom in mid-spring. Plant outside in temperate regions, in perfectly drained, light soil, 4" deep. Give full sun. Pot up where cold.

**6.** Tigridias are easy from seed. Natives of Mexico and Peru, they are not hardy outside in cold climates. Plant 4"-6" deep in rich, sandy loam, give plenty of water during the growing season, and lift after flowering. Store through winter in dry sand.

# SHRUBS AND TREES

Shrubs and trees form the backbone of a garden, and must always be planted with an eye to the future. The diversity of plant material herein listed is proof of the wide range of climatic conditions and types of soil found in Western gardens. Our attempt here has been to consider as much as is practical those finer and improved varieties or species of shrubs and trees which will inevitably take the place of some of the older types. The general information under "Garden Techniques," such as Shrubs, Trees, Fertilizers, Pruning, etc., will be found especially helpful.

# AZALEA AND RHODODENDRON

**1.** Azaleas and rhododendrons are among the most outstanding of all shrubs, distinguished by magnificent flowers and handsome form and foliage. Their culture demands and deserves especial attention. They grow best in cool climates with abundant rainfall.

**4.** Never use lime, bonemeal, or woodash. Two special fertilizers recommended for acid-tolerant plants are aluminum sulphate and cottonseed meal. New formulas have been offered by experts, but many growers still recommend well rotted manure.

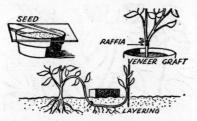

**2.** Rhododendrons are usually propagated by means of grafting. Both rhododendrons and azaleas can be grown from seed (a slow method) and by layers. Evergreen azaleas are also propagated by cuttings of half-ripe wood in summer. These are rooted in a mixture of sand and peat with some bottom heat.

**5.** A mixture of loam, leafmold, decayed manure and a little sand, placed around the base of the shrubs in fall or spring, is recommended. Never disturb the surface roots by stirring the soil. Water thoroughly after flowering to stimulate new growth.

**3.** Soil for rhododendrons and azaleas must be deep, rich in leafy humus, lime-free (or acid). Except for some of the deciduous azaleas, the position for these shrubs should be shady. Hot afternoon sun is especially to be avoided. The only pruning necessary is that of removing seedpods.

**6.** Summer drought is harmful to azaleas and rhododendrons. A heavy mulch of pine or redwood needles or any other acid leaves will help to reduce evaporation and provide a cool, protective covering for roots.

# CALIFORNIA NATIVES

**1.** The arctostaphylos or manzanitas are propagated in the same way as ceanothi. While their flowers are not so striking as those of the ceanothi, being soft pink or white, their foliage is an attractive grey-green, their trunks and branches particularly striking. "Japanesque" describes their angular shapes.

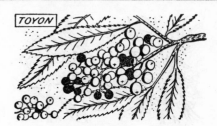

**4.** The Toyon *(Photinia arbutifolia)* is a familiar sight on California hillsides and in gardens. It can be grown from seed and will, if given normal care, thrive in almost any location. It berries heavier in full sun, but will also grow in partial shade. Keep the centers open by pruning.

**2.** *Carpenteria californica* is easily grown from seed. It is one of the best California natives for use in gardens. In its natural habitat, it grows in full sun and in dry soil, but it seems to thrive with water and partial shade under cultivation. It is covered in summer with large golden-centered white flowers.

**5.** The madrone *(Arbutus menziesi)* is one of California's most magnificent native trees. Specimens have been known to grow to 100', though 40'-50' are more usual. Their bark and shape are similar to manzanita *(Arctostaphylos manzanita)*, and their cultural needs are the same. Give acid, leafy soil, good drainage.

**3.** The fremontias *(F. californica* and *F. californica* var. *mexicana)* are probably among the best known of the native shrubs. Propagate from seed sown in sand and prick out into pots. The most usual cause of failure is poor drainage, overwatering, disturbance of roots. Prune to keep centers open. Give full sun.

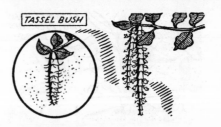

**6.** *Garrya elliptica* has the common name of Silk Tassel Bush, owing to its long silky catkins. Perhaps its greatest asset is its handsome dark-green foliage with rather wavy margins. They grow in stony, gravelly soil, which means that they require unusually good drainage. They like partial shade and cool summers.

# CAMELLIA

**1.** The camellia ranks with the azalea and rhododendron as a choice and dignified shrub. Its dark, glossy foliage is an asset, which alone makes it worth growing. The fact that it bears waxlike blooms of almost unreal perfection makes it doubly valuable.

PICK OFF HERE—LEAVING SIDE GROWTH—

**4.** The growth surrounding the bud is next year's flowering wood. It is therefore necessary to retain this when picking camellias. Frequently after a frost, when there is some drought, camellias will drop their buds. Water to offset this result.

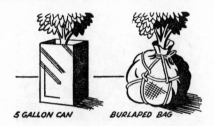

5 GALLON CAN     BURLAPED BAG

**2.** When buying camellias in the nursery, do not look for the plant with the greatest number of buds or blossoms. Rather note its general condition, its shapeliness and branching habits, vigor of growth and freedom from any pest or disease.

**5.** Camellias are excellent shrubs for formal positions, particularly on the east side of a house or wall. They also make handsome plants for large pots or tubs placed at important points, such as the sides of doorways, or in patios.

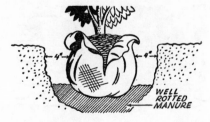

WELL ROTTED MANURE

**3.** Camellias should be planted in holes very much larger than the size of the ball requires. Mix well-rotted manure with good topsoil and place in the bottom of the hole. The addition of peat to the soil around the ball is also good.

**6.** There is also *Camellia sasanqua*, a semi-climbing or sprawling type. It is best espaliered against walls or buildings (east or north exposure). It is effective when well grown and combines well with *Rynchospermum (Trachelospermum) jasminoides*, the fragrant vine.

# CEANOTHUS

**1.** There is every good reason why any Westerner should grow ceanothus, if he can at all give them the position and conditions they require. From tip to tip of California, in dry and moist locations, one finds these shrubs or trees almost infinite in variety.

**2.** Ceanothi can be propagated from cuttings of half-ripened wood, taken sometime between July or August and October, made 3"-4" long, and placed in sharp sand. The rim of a pot is considered a good place to root these, and many other cuttings. Keep them close by covering with a bell jar or other glass.

**3.** Ceanothi are easily crossed, and one is apt to get a great variety from what he believes to be seed of only one species. But this makes it all the more interesting, and this is the way choice varieties are born. Soaking the seed in boiling water (let the seeds remain until the water cools) seems to help germination.

**4.** Almost all natives transplant badly. Early transplanting of seedlings is advantageous. Plant in small pots or cans and when once established, take care not to overwater. Rainwater is good. Prepare the soil far in advance. Plant them out before fall rains. Then give them periodic attention until established.

**5.** Ceanothi need natural settings. Slopes, banks, and informal shrubbery borders are good positions. They combine well with other natives, with pines, redwoods, madrones, huckleberry and manzanita. Spraying for mealy bug, their most common enemy, is often necessary Washing off with the hose helps.

**6.** The prostrate ceanothi are probably more admired than the upright species. Most of them are small and glossy leaved; colors vary from white to pale and deep blues and purples. They are frequently found in nature growing with dwarf manzanitas (*Arctostaphylos*), and no combination can surpass this.

# CISTUS

**1.** The cistus or rockroses are mostly natives of the Mediterranean region, and are well suited to California, where summers are warm and winters not too wet or cold. They vary in height from 8′ to dwarf types 1′ to 2′ high.

**4.** Perfect drainage is necessary. Aside from this, no special soil requirements beyond a somewhat limey, not too heavy soil are necessary. In fact, if anything, they do not want to be favored with manures or rich foods. They love plenty of sun.

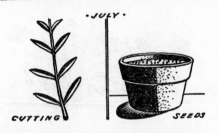

**2.** They can be propagated from cuttings made during July and August. Use non-flowering side shoots and place them in sand, providing a glass covering, if possible. It is also possible to increase them by layering.

**5.** For the gardener with a sunny slope, cistus has a special significance and value. Once established, it will thrive through hot summers and drought, with little care aside from an occasional cutting back when it becomes sprawly or badly shaped.

**3.** Cistus are quite easily grown from seed, picked as soon as ripe and sown in a mixture of light loam, sand and peat. Prick them out quite early into small pots, for they transplant badly and want as little root disturbance as possible.

**6.** There are several low varieties which are excellent for the rock garden, the top of a rock wall or as a subshrub planting for some taller material. Cistus may be had in white, several shades of pink, and rose, as well as some with blotches or markings.

# COTONEASTER

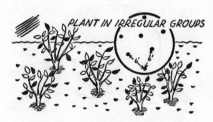

**1.** In autumn, when flowers fade and leaves fall, berried shrubs come into their own. The most satisfactory cotoneasters are evergreen, and there are many recent introductions worth planting. One may have them in upright and prostrate forms.

**2.** Anyone who has observed the ease with which cotoneasters seed themselves in the garden, knows that they can be grown from seed, sown in late spring. Most of them can also be propagated by means of layers and cuttings, taken in summer and given some bottom heat.

**3.** Pot up seedlings while they are still quite small; their roots grow rapidly and resent disturbance. When they have reached the 3" or 4" pot size, it is quite safe to plant them out in well prepared ground. Plant with moist peat in the hole.

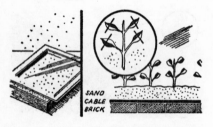

PLANT IN IRREGULAR GROUPS

**4.** Cotoneasters, like their thorned relatives, the pyracanthas, make bright spots in the shrubbery border. Among the upright types, *C. francheti*, *C. harroviana*, *C. salicifolia floccosa* and *C. dielsiana* are good varieties. Where space permits, plant them in groups of 3 or 5.

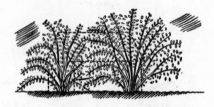

**5.** Both cotoneasters and pyracanthas are frequently used for informal hedges and for blocking out or screening. Some pruning is necessary to keep their centers open and weak, twiggy growth eliminated. Never top them; this destroys their graceful, arching habit.

**6.** Some of the choicest of cotoneasters are prostrate and are excellent for ground covers, rock gardens and walls, subshrub plantings and parking strips. *C. adpressa*, *C. praecox*, *C. microphylla thymifolia* and *C. pannosa nana* are good varieties. Watch for scale and black aphis.

# DAPHNE

**1.** It seems impossible to mention daphne *(D. odora)* without first speaking of its fragrance, so potent that a small sprig of this flowering shrub can perfume a large room. The daphne, however, is more than just a fragrant shrub; it is handsome, too.

CUTTINGS · SEED · LAYERING

**2.** *Daphne odora*, hardy in California, is propagated in 3 ways: by means of cuttings, taken in June or July, with or without a heel and rooted in sand or water; occasionally by seed under glass; and by layers, made in early summer and not removed until at least 1 year later.

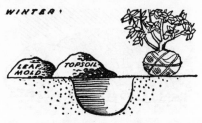

WINTER

**3.** The soil for daphnes should be deep, well drained, rich in humus and slightly acid. Morning sun and afternoon shade are best. Plant from late fall to early spring. They can be planted when in bloom if taken with a large ball and planted as carefully as one would a camellia or rhododendron.

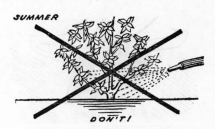

SUMMER

DON'T!

**4.** A daphne requires little or no pruning. As a rule, one prunes it when picking flowers. Select lateral shoots; the leader (center stem) is needed for future growth. A rest period after flowering is necessary. Do not overwater in summer. Increase watering in fall. Overwatering results in poor flowering.

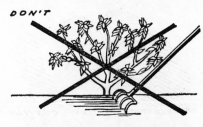

DON'T

**5.** It is a mistake to cultivate around the roots of daphne. Treat it as the rhododendron. Give it a summer mulch of leaves, peat or pine needles. Do not plant smaller plants requiring cultivating near its stem. Daphnes are choice enough to stand alone.

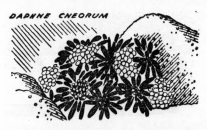

DAPHNE CNEORUM

**6.** There are two other daphnes fairly commonly grown. Both are suited to cold climates, and so are found in eastern and northern gardens. *Daphne mezereum* is a deciduous, upright type with dark lavender flowers. *Daphne cneorum* is a rock garden gem, small, tiny leaved and covered with pink blooms.

# FUCHSIA

**1.** The fuchsia is one of the most adaptable shrubs in cultivation. Most hybrid varieties prefer cool, moist climates, but there are a few species which will grow under fairly hot, dry conditions if given plenty of water at the roots.

**4.** The standard fuchsia (see Fuchsia Pruning for method of growing) is as useful in its place as the standard rose. Use it for accent along shaded paths, at the corners of beds, to accent a garden accessory, or in large pots or tubs at the sides of entrances.

PROPAGATION BY CUTTINGS

**2.** Though fuchsias can be grown from seed, the most usual method is by cuttings. They are made in spring of young shoots which develop after the early spring pruning. A rooting medium will hasten their growth (see Hormones and Cuttings).

**5.** Fuchsias are as attractive as trailing begonias when grown in hanging baskets. They have the added advantage of a long period of bloom and ease of culture. One variety, *autumnale*, has beautifully colored foliage which is quite as decorative as flowers.

**3.** The ordinary bush fuchsia can be trained to grow in espalier form. For this purpose, select a tall-growing variety, choose well placed side branches for fastening to the wall or trellis, and remove those not required. Then pinch back shoots on these lateral stems to produce abundant flowering.

**6.** There are fuchsias for growing in rock gardens, rock walls and at the sides of pools, also. Most of them, such as *Fuchsia procumbens*, have small leaves and flowers, and are so dainty that they should not be planted near greedy, spreading plants.

# FUCHSIA PRUNING

**1.** Fuchsias should be pruned with the locality in which they are grown and the purpose for which they are being used kept constantly in mind. Prune in spring after frosts. Earlier pruning may result in killing or damaging young growth which always follows cutting back.

**2.** It is necessary to select certain varieties of fuchsias for special purposes, such as for standards or hanging baskets. When a rounded, bushy fuchsia is desired (this is the most useful form for bedding and shrubbery borders) pinch back the side growths. This will result in heavier bloom.

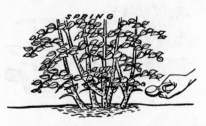

**3.** To keep the fuchsia bushy and compact, all branches are cut back to within 2 or 3 buds of the main stem. Also cut out all dead, crossing and spindly growth. Make cuts clean and leave no ugly stubs. Pruning is an art to be practiced with care and skill.

**4.** Standard fuchsias are pruned by removing all branches from the main stem from the ground up to the height desired, usually 4' to 5'. Keep all buds rubbed off below that point. Pinch back top growth in spring; a full, rounded head results. A heavier pruning is given in autumn or early spring.

**5.** One of the most attractive forms in which the fuchsias can be grown is the espalier. Select well placed stems, tie to a wall or fence and eliminate stems not required. For a high espalier, cut back at the bottom; if a low espalier, the top is pruned back. Keep sideshoots along the main stems back to 2 or 3 buds.

**6.** Fuchsias are attractive as cut flowers. They are not very good "keepers," but some find they last longer if the stems are burned or plunged into hot water. They are difficult to arrange while on a stem; the most effective method is to let the individual flowers float in a flat dish or bowl.

# GARDENIA

**1.** The gardenia, or Cape Jasmine, is confused with the camellia, which it resembles. The gardenia, however, has an exotic fragrance, is smaller and less hardy than the camellia. While the camellia is superseding the gardenia in popularity, this plant still has its place, especially in warm climates.

REMOVE THIS BUD

ALLOW ONLY ONE BUD IN ONE AXIL

**4.** The gardenia is usually allowed only one bud to a leaf axil, while the camellia may have as many as 2 or 3. Disbudding causes larger flowers and is also said to promote greater fragrance in the gardenia, which blooms most of the year.

DIAMETER 10"

**2.** Propagation is by cuttings in winter, 3" long (or with 3-4 buds) in clean, sharp sand. Keep close in a propagating case or place in a pot which can be covered with a bell jar. Bottom heat is required to keep the temperature of 70° needed for proper rooting. When rooting begins, admit some air.

**5.** Outdoors, the gardenia grows best in partial shade and in peaty, leafy soil, which can be kept damp, but not wet. Gardenias are shallow rooted; do not cultivate near roots. They can also be grown in tubs and large pots, a safe method for colder climates, and for those with greenhouses and conservatories.

⅔ RICH LOAM
⅓ ROTTED COW MANURE
A LITTLE SAND

DIAMETER OF POT 4"

**3.** Well rooted cuttings are then potted up into a mixture of loam, decayed manure and sand. This is a fairly heavy compost, needed for a firm potting and to prevent drying out. Drainage is essential. Pot on as the plants grow, but still keep them in a warm temperature (65° at night).

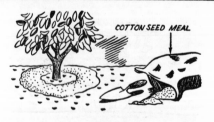

COTTON SEED MEAL

**6.** The gardenia, like the camellia, is fond of food and can be given occasional feedings. Aside from top dressings of well rotted manure when buds form, they can be fed with bonemeal or cottonseed meal.

# HELIANTHEMUM

**1.** Helianthemums are rightly called Sun Roses, for they love warmth and light and their flowers close in dull or dark weather. They are hardy, of easy culture, and will stand some drought and neglect. Their color range is extensive — from white, through pinks, reds, yellows and oranges.

**4.** Helianthemums may also be used for edgings to sunny beds, in perennial borders and as low plantings in front of shrubbery. They combine well with cistus, which they resemble in miniature form, and enjoy the same cultural treatment. Use masses of 1 color or harmonizing colors.

· CUTTINGS ·

**2.** They can be grown from seed, cuttings and division. Propagation from cuttings of green wood in spring or fall is simplest and fastest. In 6 weeks the cuttings will be ready to pot up or put into flats. In another 6 weeks or 2 months, plant out.

**5.** The dry rock garden or rock wall makes a happy home for helianthemums. The rocks will afford some protection to their roots, so that even a hot exposure will not injure them. On the other hand, helianthemums enjoy the cool summers of the San Francisco Bay region, though sun is necessary.

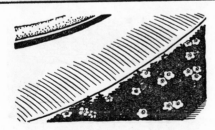

**3.** The problem of what to plant in parking strips or as a ground cover in a hot location frequently confronts us. Masses of helianthemums, planted 12"-18" apart, will answer the need. They spread rapidly and require a yearly cutting back. After cutting back, top dress with compost.

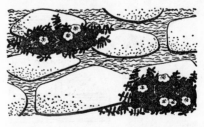

**6.** Their prostrate habit makes them good for planting among stepping stones and joints of pavings. In all plantings, drainage and light, not-too-rich soil should be provided. They are not long lived and must be replaced every few years.

# HYDRANGEA

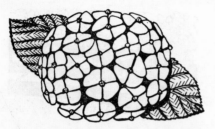

**1.** The hydrangea still remains one of the showiest and most useful shrubs grown in California gardens, and elsewhere in greenhouses. The species *H. hortensis*, with its large pink or white trusses of flowers, is a good choice for a general shrub in a partly shaded position.

SUMMER

**4.** The newly potted plants can be summered in frames or lathhouses, where they can enjoy cool conditions. Young plants are often planted out the first summer, but unless they are strongly rooted, and after-planting care is regular, wait until the following spring.

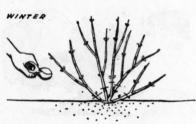

WINTER

**2.** Hydrangeas can be cut back in autumn or spring, depending on the climate. Hard pruning (6" from the ground) results in large, handsome flowers the following summer, but produces rather weak stems. A more shapely, straight-stemmed bush results from light pruning.

TO MAKE THEM BLUE

ALUM

IRON SHAVINGS

**5.** How to make hydrangeas blue? Add alum in some form (aluminum sulphate, applied at the rate of 1 lb. or less to 1 sq. yd., is good) or iron shavings, and work in around the roots. New hybrids, particularly the French, have been added to hydrangea collections. These include shades of pink, rose and carmine.

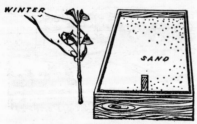

WINTER

SAND

**3.** Make cuttings of half-ripened wood at the time of pruning and place in moist sand. Some bottom heat will hasten rooting. Rooted cuttings are potted up in early spring or summer, depending on when cuttings were made. Use 2 parts loam, 1 part leafmold, 1 part sand, ½ part rotted cow manure and a little bonemeal.

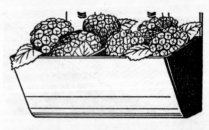

**6.** Hydrangeas respond to generous feeding and watering, particularly before coming into bloom. If using them as cut flowers, cut stems the evening before and plunge them into deep, cold water overnight. Sprinkle a little water over their heads, also.

# MATILIJA POPPY

**1.** The Matilija poppy, or California Tree Poppy, is a stunning perennial native to California and Mexico. Large, white, papery-petaled, golden-centered flowers bloom through summer into late fall. They require plenty of warmth, good drainage. Avoid root disturbance.

**4.** It seems almost proverbial that plants hard to start are as hard to remove once well established. This is to an extent true of the Matilija poppy, whose deep, firmly set roots stubbornly defy moving. After the poppies have bloomed and leaves begin to yellow, cut to the ground.

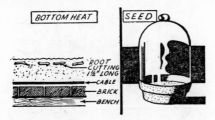

**2.** Propagation is by division of roots in autumn, by seed sown in seed pans, covered with glass and given some bottom heat until germinated. Root cuttings, taken 1½" long, and also given bottom heat, are also possible. Seedlings are taprooted; prick out into pots when quite small.

**5.** The only time when Matilija poppies can be lifted, divided and replanted is in autumn, when they are most dormant. Even so, transplant almost immediately, for the roots dry rapidly. Have the ground thoroughly prepared and use no manure.

**3.** Both seedlings and root cuttings are then grown on either in pots or cans until planted out in the garden. Do not allow roots to penetrate far through the bottoms of the containers. Breaking of roots will result in some shock to the plants and might cause failure.

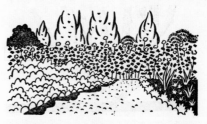

**6.** Owners of small gardens will be wise to forego planting the Matilija poppy, which grows to 8' and spreads as wide. It is possible to grow them in 5-gallon cans sunk in the ground. In any case, keep them well in the background where they will not interfere with less vigorous neighbors.

# ROSE CULTURE

**1.** Roses are propagated by 4 methods: *Seed,* usually to produce stock; *cuttings,* taken between October and December, placed in a box, nursery bed or coldframe, and usually lifted in about 6 months; *budding,* the usual method; *layering,* especially of climbing roses.

**4.** Summer pruning is light and is carried out in August. Cut back all stems that have flowered to within about 2 buds of the main stem. After pruning, a feeding with balanced commercial fertilizer, followed by a thorough watering, will send roses into a good second bloom lasting well into autumn.

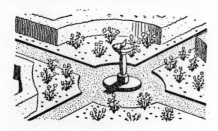

**2.** Roses require an open, sunny position (unless grown in very hot districts, where afternoon shade is desirable), good soil, adequate drainage and plenty of food. As a rule, roses lend themselves to formal planting and are best kept in an important, though not constantly viewed, part of the garden scheme.

**5.** Rose growers and fanciers say that one can hardly overfeed roses. An early spring feeding with bonemeal or commercial fertilizer helps to send them off into fresh growth. Repeat after the summer pruning. A winter mulch of manure is put on directly following the winter pruning.

**3.** Prune December to late February in California, March or April in the East and colder parts of the West. Prune hybrid tea roses to 3 or 4 canes, on which 3 buds (or eyes) are left. Less severe pruning will retain 5 to 7 canes (stems) and 6 to 7 buds. Cut to outside buds.

**6.** Dormant and delayed dormant sprayings prevent fungous diseases such as mildew and rust. Spray often during the growing season to prevent ravages by various pests (see Pests). Disbud to produce roses of large size and perfect form. Little disbudding is required if quantity, rather than quality, is desired.

# ROSE PLANTING

**1.** The fact that roses will grow under various conditions and in many types of soil should not lessen one's effort to give them the best of care. This means starting with proper planting. Examine bushes upon arrival from the nursery. If dry, soak in water for a day or two, or heel into the ground.

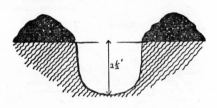

**2.** Dig a large hole, at least 2½′ deep and as wide. Break up hard soil in the bottom and add coarse drainage material, if necessary. Put in 6″ of rotted manure, then a layer of topsoil. If the subsoil is unusually heavy, the addition of gypsum will help break it up.

**3.** Before planting, look carefully for bruised roots and branches. Prune back cleanly beyond any breaks, always making root-cuts slanting on the underside, and cuts on branches to an outside bud. This is to insure roots growing downward and new topgrowth outward.

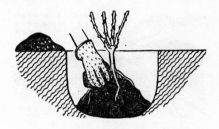

**4.** A cone-shaped mound in the center of the hole will form a perfect base on which the circle of roots can rest. Plant so that the bud and stock union (forming a swelling on the stem) is just even with the surface of the soil. Firm the soil around the small roots with the hand.

**5.** A little bonemeal can be thrown in at this point. After the roots are covered and the hole is ¾ full, tamp down the soil with the ball of the foot. Leave a basin 6″ deep so that plenty of water can be given to the newly planted rose.

**6.** In a few days, after the soaked soil has settled, fill in the basin with loose topsoil. In cold districts a mulch of straw or leaves should be put on after planting, which is usually done in early autumn or spring.

# SHRUBS, EVERGREEN

**1.** The red and yellow strawberrylike fruits and small, white, bell-shaped flowers of the *Arbutus unedo* appear together in autumn. Attractive green foliage, hardiness, neat habit and freedom from any serious pest or disease, make this shrub, Strawberry Tree, worth growing. Give it good soil, plenty of water.

**2.** Quite frequently a shrub is needed to fill a narrow, high space which is shady or partly shady. *Azara microphylla*, tall, slender, delicately textured and dark green, will fill that need. It needs an immediate background, and is best when stenciled against a wall.

**3.** One of the most attractive of the barberries is *Berberis Darwini*, a medium-sized shrub which has small, glossy, hollylike leaves, orange flowers in spring and dark blue berries in the fall. It is a good middle border shrub, and combines well with Oregon Grape (*Mahonia aquifolium*).

**4.** Gardeners and landscape architects are always on the lookout for permanent low and medium-height evergreen shrubs. Such is *Raphiolepis indica rosea*, a fairly recent introduction and much improved over *R. indica*. Its spring flowers are an apple-blossom pink, its foliage beautiful.

**5.** *Mahonia aquifolium* (Oregon Grape) is not a new shrub, but it is still considered one of the best medium-height shrubs for shrubbery borders and foundation planting in shade or part shade. Combine it with dwarf mahonias and with *Photinia serrulata* (Chinese Toyon), a taller, bronzy-leaved shrub.

**6.** The Japanese Pittosporum (*Pittosporum tobira*) is shunned by some who think it is "common." Frequent use has not made it less valuable as a reliable shrub for foundation planting, for background and as a specimen. It can be grown from seed or cuttings. It makes beautiful arrangements.

# SHRUBS, FLOWERING

**1.** Deciduous flowering shrubs comprise a large class and require special culture. They are therefore worthy of particular attention. Spirea, deutzia, philadelphus, diervilla, and forsythia belong in this group. All of them flower in spring on wood formed during the previous summer.

**4.** Move deciduous shrubs during their dormant, or leafless period, November-January, or early February. Then lift and replant without a ball of earth around roots (or on bare-root). They should, however, be planted with as much care as though in active growth.

**2.** Most of them form suckers which can be planted. Propagate by hardwood cuttings in late summer or fall. Make them pencil-thick, 8" long. Cut below the node; cut clean with a sharp knife. Bury cuttings in the ground a month or so, or set them outside in a sand-bottomed trench.

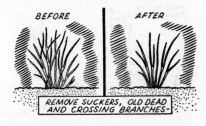

**5.** All pruning should be practiced with the shape of the shrub or tree in mind. The natural habit of most flowering shrubs is arching, open, graceful, slightly irregular. Do not top. Cut out weak, crossing, old or dead wood and tip back new (next year's flowering) wood only when needed to balance growth.

**3.** By the following autumn, 1 year later, the cuttings will probably have rooted enough to be lifted and potted up into cans or good-sized pots. Let them grow on until the next year, by which time they should be well enough established to stand planting out into their permanent places.

**6.** Flowering shrubs are never so lovely as when used as massed planting along a lawn, drive or walk. Plant in groups, keeping the various species together, with enough space between to give each shrub opportunity for full development, yet close enough to give a massed, abundant effect.

# SHRUBS, SIX GREY

*SENECIO GREYI·*

**1.** Grey tones have a very real value and an important place in the garden. They have been called harmonizers and peacemakers, because of their happy faculty of making clashing colors agree. One of the most handsome of the grey shrubs is *Senecio greyi*. It grows 3′-4′ tall, and has interesting leaves.

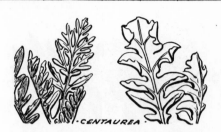

*·CENTAUREA·*

**4.** There are many centaureas, ranging from those 1′ high to others 3′ or more. *Centaurea ragusina* (probably known under other names as well), is a low compact plant not over 10″, 12″ high, and very striking. Use it toward the front of the border or for bedding solidly with pink, blue, soft yellow, red or white.

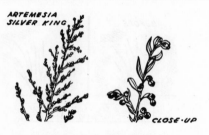

ARTEMESIA
SILVER KING

*CLOSE·UP*

**2.** Artemesia Silver King offers a contrast to *Senecio greyi*. This herbaceous perennial has a delicate texture and graceful, upright habit. It is one of the best of its class for the mixed border, its silvery leaves softening harsh reds or oranges and blending with blues and lavenders.

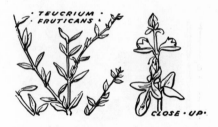

·TEUCRIUM·
·FRUTICANS·

*CLOSE·UP·*

**5.** *Teucrium fruticans* grows to full shrub size, 8′-10′ tall, but can be kept lower by pruning back. It is easily propagated by cuttings, and quickly grows into an attractive grey-white, fine-leaved shrub with small lavender flowers. It is hardy in all but very low temperatures.

·DUSTY MILLER·
·SENECIO CINERARIA·

**3.** *Senecio cineraria*, better known as Dusty Miller, is a truly old-fashioned plant, shunned by some modern gardeners. Now that greys are coming into their own, this standby is returning to favor; 2′ to 3′ tall and almost as wide, it is good in the border, or used with geraniums or some similar plant.

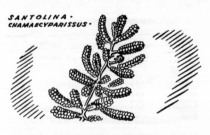

SANTOLINA·
CHAMAECYPARISSUS·

**6.** Also in grandmother's garden, probably around her geranium or amaryllis (belladonna) beds was santolina. A stiff, compact habit makes it useful for formal edgings and bedding. It is hardy, grown from cuttings and best renewed every 4 or 5 years.

# TREES, DECIDUOUS

**1.** In fall, the Maidenhair Tree (*Ginkgo biloba*) resembles a golden cloud with a carpet of gold beneath it. Though quite slow-growing, it rewards those who plant it. Give it an open, specimen position, with no close neighbors to detract from its beauty. It wants a deep, rich soil and much water.

**4.** One may tell the Scarlet Oak from the Red Oak, with which it is frequently confused, by the narrower, more acutely lobed leaves, by the more brilliant coloring, the more angular, less rounded habit of growth, and by the fact that its leaves do not adhere so long. Both these oaks stand some drought.

**2.** The Liquidamber, or Sweet Gum, is one of the few autumn-colored trees that seems to rival those in the East. Its maplelike leaves appear like many-colored stars in October and November. It is a slender, angularly branched tree, and is lovely either etched against the sky or a group of dark pines.

**5.** Poplars have suffered some unpopularity, owing to the fact that they have been improperly placed in many gardens. Never plant them in the garden proper, for their roots travel far and are greedy and tenacious. In the background, their spirelike tops etched against the sky, they lend atmosphere.

**3.** The Red Oak (*Quercus rubra*) is distinguished by its large lobed leaves which become very dark in autumn and which adhere to the branches long after every other deciduous tree has lost its leaves. It becomes, in time, a handsome, round-headed tree, excellent for shade or street purposes.

**6.** The Tulip Tree (*Liriodendron tulipfera*) is so-called because of its greenish-yellow tuliplike flowers in spring. Its botanical name derives from the lyre-shaped leaves which are soft blue-green and shade giving. A native of the eastern U. S., it will, with sufficient water and deep soil, thrive in the West.

# TREES, FLOWERING

**1.** Anyone who has seen *Magnolia soulangeana* in all the glory of full spring bloom will probably not rest until he, too, has one in his garden. It is propagated by seed, layering, budding and grafting. Plant in an open position (it grows well on lawns); provide drainage; mulch every 2 years with manure.

**4.** Flowering dogwood symbolizes the loveliness of spring to those who have seen it growing in the wild. It thrives under the protective shade of tall forest trees, and in moist, leafy soil. The species is white flowered, but there is also a red-flowered form. Both have brightly colored leaves in autumn.

**2.** The name Long-Clustered Goldenchain is enough to make any inquisitive gardener stop and consider. This small tree, a member of the Pea family, bears in spring long racemes of flowers which look exactly like yellow wisteria. Of rather light texture, it needs some background to be completely effective.

**5.** One sees few tree wisterias. Few nurseries offer them and then at fairly high prices. But on lawns, or near pools, with no other planting nearby, they offer more than a dozen less rare shrubs or trees. They are grafted on stems about 4' high and spread 3 times their height.

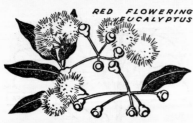

**3.** From Australia come the eucalypti, among them many small flowering types of highly ornamental character. *E. ficifolia*, the Scarlet Flowering Gum and *E. leucoxylon rosea* are two of the most outstanding, and bloom in winter and early spring. They are hardy down to 20° of frost.

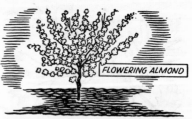

**6.** Flowering fruit trees are easily and quickly grown. One can have them in bloom from the first of the year to late May. One of the first to bloom is Flowering Almond. One of the loveliest is the dainty double-flowered white, ideal for small gardens, delightful with small spring-flowering bulbs planted underneath.

# TREES, FRUIT

**1.** Most fruit trees require deep, rich loam to produce a good quality of fruit. Certain districts grow some fruits better than others, and it is well to be informed if one is planting many trees. Order trees early from a reliable nursery and plant as soon as trees are available. usually between January and March.

**4.** Fruit trees are pruned to produce a well shaped tree of productive and vigorous character. Prune late where heavy frosts are prevalent. Spur prune apricots, apples, pears, some plums and sweet cherries. Long pruning is practiced on peaches, nectarines, figs and almonds, whose fruit appears on the new wood.

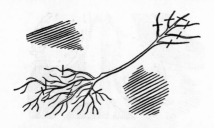

**2.** Young trees are always pruned before being planted. In order to maintain a balance between roots and top, both tops and roots are pruned. Prune back the main stem to about 2'. Then tip back the lateral branches or stems, most or some of which are kept to form future side branches.

**5.** A delayed dormant spraying at the time the buds swell is necessary to control leaf curl on peaches, pear blight, brown rot on apricots and shot-hole fungus on several kinds of fruits. Bordeaux mixture is commonly used; the addition of lead arsenate or nicotine sulphate helps to control certain harmful pests.

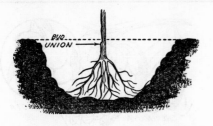

**3.** Plant the tree, which is usually 2 years old, to the same depth as it was in the nursery. The bud (or union of stock and scion) should be level or slightly below the surface of the soil. Make a deep hole, spread roots and plant straight, unless planting into a prevailing wind; 20'-25' apart is usual for most trees.

**6.** Thin to produce fruit of good size and to prevent rotting of fruit, as, brown rot on apricots. Thin apricots to 4"-5" apart, apples, pears and peaches to 5"-6". Small fruits, such as plums, are thinned to 1". Some growers wait to thin apples until the fruit is large enough to be of some use.

# TREES, SUBTROPICAL FRUIT

ORANGE
LEMON
GRAPEFRUIT

**1.** Citrus fruits want good, deep loam, plenty of water, excellent drainage. Excessive lime is harmful. Oranges stand quite severe frost. The lemon is less hardy. It fruits all year, is found to have a thinner skin and more juice if ripened off the tree. Grapefruit demands the same culture as the orange.

**4.** The avocado grows best in the mild sections of the citrus belt. Its particular needs are: humidity, mild winters, moderate summer heat, good drainage, rich loam. Mixed plantings are needed for pollination. Shallow roots are injured by cultivating. Little pruning is required, just some thinning out.

**2.** The loquat is coming back into favor as an ornamental tree. Espaliered, grown in tubs or in raised tree wells in patios or on terraces, it is handsome with its large, bold, dark-green leaves. Its fruit is also good. Give it plenty of water.

**5.** *Feijoa sellowiana* (Pineapple Guava), an attractive grey-leaved shrub that bears interesting red and grey flowers, is grown in many California gardens as an ornamental shrub. It wants good soil and ordinary care and is hardy to 5° of frost. Its small, pear-shaped, green fruits are excellent for jelly and preserves.

**3.** An old olive tree can be one of the most picturesque trees grown. It is also beautiful while still quite young. It is best in fairly warm districts, but is by no means a tender tree. Deep soil, generous watering until established and some pruning until well shaped are required.

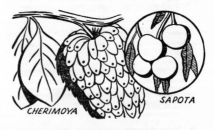

CHERIMOYA
SAPOTA

**6.** Only those in mild-winter districts can grow the Cherimoya, which is hardy to 25°. It makes a large, handsome tree and its large, green, heart-shaped fruits are ambrosial in flavor. Many predict it will in time become a favorite among the more unusual winter fruits. Same culture as for citrus fruits.

# SPECIAL PLANTS

Gardening is becoming less trial-and-error and more of a science. No longer do we plant something and hope it will grow. We try to learn beforehand the special requirements of a plant and give it the conditions under which it will thrive. In line with this new approach to gardening, we offer "Special Plants" for special places, covering a range that takes us from the sunny South to the cool, moist North. Use the "Garden Techniques" section for general facts which may apply to these plants.

# CACTI AND SUCCULENTS

**1.** Cacti and succulents are mostly natives of the southwestern U. S. and Mexico, whose main requirements are heat, drainage and little water. There are 2 groups of succulents, that composed of plants which store water and another comprising those which are drought resisting.

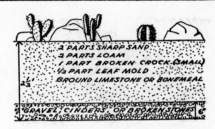

**4.** The soil for succulents (including cacti) should, as the diagram indicates, contain porous material, and no organic matter, which causes rotting. If planting a cactus or succulent garden in a position where the soil is generally heavy, remove it to the depth of 3' and fill with drainage material and light soil.

**2.** Most cacti and succulents are easy to propagate. Sow larger-seeded species in light sandy soil, with a top layer of fine sifted charcoal; cover with glass. While not allowed to be completely dry, they should never be kept very wet. Sterilize soil and disinfect seed. Prick out young seedlings into thumb pots.

**5.** Cacti and succulents are so individual and often so fantastic, even grotesque, that they are best kept to themselves. This has a cultural advantage, as well, since they demand such special conditions. Any placing of rocks should facilitate, rather than hinder, drainage facilities.

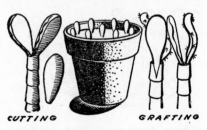

CUTTING       GRAFTING

**3.** Leaves or joints which fall off succulents frequently root on the soil surface, either in pots or in the garden. This indicates that they can be grown from cuttings, which, in the case of succulents, should be allowed to dry out for a few days before being inserted into sand. Grafting is another method of propagation.

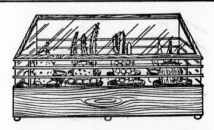

**6.** A sunny window, glass case or any light, warm spot will make a home for succulents. Often overlooked by the amateur is the winter rest, when water should be given at rare intervals (once a week). Succulents grown indoors all winter benefit by being placed outdoors in summer.

# FERNS

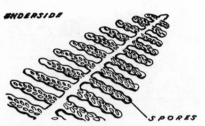

**1.** Examine the back of a fern leaf, or frond, as it is properly called and you will find it dotted with powdery brown bodies which some have timidly confessed they thought were scales! Actually, they are spore cases which contain the spores (generative cells) from which new ferns are propagated.

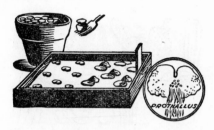

**4.** In a few weeks the prothalli, tiny heart-shaped membranes, will have grown large enough to prick out into flats. Equal portions of light loam and leafmold, with the addition of sand, make a good compost for pricking out. As the sporelings grow, pot them up individually and continue to move them on.

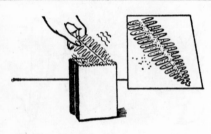

**2.** When the spore cases become ripe, they split open and the spores are set free. Place mature fronds, top side up, for a few days on a white paper in a warm, dry place. The spore cases will release the spores which can then be shaken into a bag, later to be sown. Spores resemble coarse dust.

**5.** In about a year these plants which began as minute prothalli will have grown into good-sized ferns. From then on they can be grown in pots or, if hardy, can be planted directly into some shady, moist part of the garden. There are a few species which thrive in dry locations, and even like lime.

**3.** Sow in flat seed pans in light soil mixture. Do not cover the spores. Soak the pot from below and never directly on top. A temperature of approximately 60° is right for germination. Give a little more air as the small plants, properly called prothalli, appear.

**6.** Large clumps can be lifted and divided. Some possess such firmly massed roots that it is necessary to cut through with a sharp spade. In replanting, it is well to add plenty of peat or leafmold to the hole. The best time for dividing is autumn or early spring, preferably the former.

# FRAGRANT PLANTS

**1.** Visual beauty is usually enough to make a plant valuable. If it also has fragrance, it is irresistible. *Viburnum burkwoodi*, a half-evergreen shrub of recent introduction from England, is one of this class. It grows to about 5', nearly as wide, and bears large, fragrant flowers, pink in bud, later white.

**4.** The so-called Mock Orange (some call it syringa) bloomed in front of almost every home twenty years ago, it seemed. Meet a newcomer, *Philadelphus virginal*, less rampant than old *P. coronarius*, and very choice, with large, white, fragrant flowers. Summer-blooming, it can be pruned in early fall or spring.

**2.** Many new and more spectacular shrubs and plants will appear within the next few decades, but it is doubtful that *Daphne odora* will ever be surpassed for sheer sweetness. Easterners cannot grow it, but they can have *Daphne cneorium*, a smaller though beautiful shrub, though less fragrant.

**5.** The true syringa is the lilac. Lilacs have been widely hybridized and now include almost every shade of lavender, purple, pink and white. Here is a shrub which grows best in the East and North, where cold winters prevail. Mulch them each fall with a heavy top dressing of manure. They like lime also.

**3.** Some of the lesser known species of buddleia (Butterfly Bush or Summer Lilac) are so superior to the ordinary species that they should be more widely grown. *B. asiatica, B. alternifolia*, and such varieties as Fortune, Charming and Dubonnet are a few. Hardy in most climates, they can be cut to the ground after flowering.

**6.** Heliotropes are hardy enough to grow outdoors in the South and parts of the West, but where temperatures go below 25°, they must be grown as greenhouse or pot plants. They can be bedded outside as summer annuals, for they come easily from seed in flats or broadcast outdoors.

# STRAWBERRIES

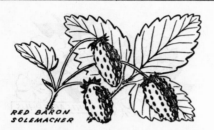

RED BARON SOLEMACHER

**1.** Most of us have seen ordinary strawberries, but how many know Strawberry Baron Solemacher, a runnerless type which is decorative enough to use as an edging in the herb or vegetable garden, in pots or strawberry jars? It is delicious, fragrant and hardy, and resembles the wild strawberry.

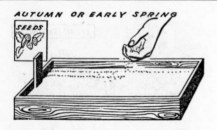

AUTUMN OR EARLY SPRING

SEEDS

**2.** This variety will bear 6 months from seed, which germinates easily. Sow in fall or early spring and plant out when they are 3"-4" high. Prepare the soil at the time you sow the seed, so that it will have time to aerate and mellow. Give them a sunny location.

**3.** If one is growing them in a large bed, it is best to plant them as one would ordinary strawberries, in hills with furrows for irrigating between. Unlike other strawberries, the Baron Solemacher requires no thinning out of runners, though it should be divided once a year.

**4.** Bright green leaves and small, glossy, pointed berries make these strawberries attractive for pots and window boxes. Give them a compost of 3 parts loam, 1 part sand, 1 part leafmold and ½ part rotted cow manure. Water generously and divide in early spring.

**5.** The Baron Solemacher is also available in a yellow-berried form, which is even more fragrant than the red, if that is possible. If planting them in strawberry jars, why not include a few of the yellow-fruited variety?

**6.** If planted out in early spring, these plants will bear in June or early July and continue up until frosts. In fact, in a Central California garden, they fruit during the frosts, though they are not so red, large, or sweet. Eat them freshly picked, plain or with cream, or honey!

# SIX VINES

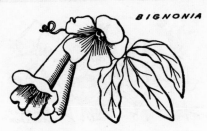

**BIGNONIA**

**1.** The bignonias, or Trumpet Vines, are dramatic and flamboyant. Not all are hardy enough to winter through colder climates, but one, *Bignonia tweediana* (Cat's Claw) will endure down to 10° frost. *Bignonia cherere*, evergreen, with large red and yellow flowers, is one of the finest and is almost everblooming.

**CONFEDERATE JASMINE · RYNCHOSPERMUM JASMINOIDES**

**4.** The Star Jasmine (*Rhynchospermum jasminoides*) has a double use, as a low-growing vine and ground cover. It has shiny, dark-green leaves and small, pinwheel-shaped, delicately fragrant flowers. It prefers partial shade and is hardy. For small archways and low walls it is superb.

**DOUBLE YELLOW JASMINE**

**· JASMINUM PRIMULINUM**

**2.** Early in spring, the fragrant double yellow jasmine graces fences and walls. It is evergreen in mild climates, half-evergreen elsewhere, and has no special cultural needs beyond a sunny location, not too heavy soil, and water. Another jasmine, *J. nudiflorum*, blooms in midwinter.

**PASSIFLORA MANICATA**

**5.** Visitors to San Francisco's Treasure Island will remember the striking red-flowered vine on the wall in the Court of Reflections. It was *Passiflora manicata*, the Scarlet Passion Vine, an evergreen, handsome-leaved climber that is hardy to about 23°. It is a strong grower.

**CLEMATIS ·**

**3.** All clematis need deep, cool, rich soil to which some lime has been added. Plant them in shade or partial shade in warm climates. Pruning depends on whether flowering takes place on old or new wood. Propagate by seed cuttings under glass layers and grafting.

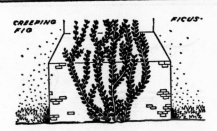

**CREEPING FIG · FICUS ·**

**6.** Almost universally used are the ivies and ficus (Creeping Fig). Various types of ivy, including small and large leaved, plain and variegated, are available. Ficus may be had in small and large-leaved forms and is unsurpassed for covering stone and brick surfaces. Both prefer some shade.

# WILDFLOWERS

**1.** Wildflowers, despite their ruggedness when growing on hillsides, on plains and in crevices, are strangely delicate when brought under cultivation. Of all plants, they can least stand handling and fussing over. Most wildflowers should be sown directly in the open ground, prepared several weeks ahead.

**2.** Just before the fall rains, while the soil is still warm, broadcast wildflower seed. Rake the ground smooth before sowing, then sow, not too thickly; gently rake in seed and, if the area is not large, cover lightly with sand. Overhead sprinklings may be necessary if rains are long delayed.

**3.** Once germination starts, sprinkling must be continued. It is fatal to allow young, shallow-rooted seedlings to dry out. In the East and North, sow California wildflowers in spring, after frosts. If the weather becomes hot, water once or twice during the growing season.

**4.** Knowing conditions under which wildlings grow in their native habitats helps us in using them. Lupins want sun, but like atmospheric moisture. Pentstemon and zauschneria want full sun and stand drought, as does also Indian Paint Brush. Delphinium and poppies like sun but root moisture.

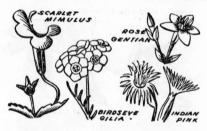

**5.** Members of the violet and gentian family like cool root runs and are found in forest or meadow. Some mimulus (Monkey flower) grow near streams; others on sunny hillsides. Wild phloxes are found in open positions and want well drained soil, as do Indian Pinks (*Silene californica* and *S. laciniata*), good rock plants.

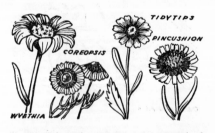

**6.** The aster family includes some of the brightest wildflowers covering a long period of bloom, early spring to late fall. These early asters are mostly bright yellow and bloom with spring's first warm days. All are excellent for naturalizing in open fields and along roadsides.

# SPECIAL GARDENS

Not all of us can have a water garden
or a rock garden, but at least we like
to know how they are made. Our purpose here is to cover, simply and
without bewildering detail, some of
the subjects which we could not
correctly mention in other sections.
Again, be ready to refer to "Garden
Techniques," especially when considering such special problems as Lawns
and Vegetables.

# GROUND COVERS

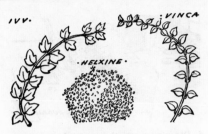

**1.** Ground covers are becoming more important, especially where lawn growing is a problem. Thymes and camomile love sun and stand some abuse; helxine wants shade and moisture; strawberry does best with a little shade and some water; *Dichondra repens* is said to be good in sun and shade and requires water.

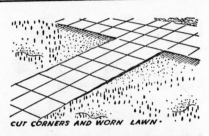

CUT CORNERS AND WORN LAWN.

**2.** Frequently a lawn will refuse to grow on certain corners. Dichondra is recommended as a lawn substitute, also *Arenaria caespitosa*, a velvety green moss. Camomile is sun loving, bright green and can be mowed as a lawn.

**3.** Heavy shade and greedy roots make lawn growing difficult under trees. *Vinca minor, Dichondra repens, Nepeta glechoma,* helxine and ivy are strong growing, hardy and evergreen. All do better with some shade and generous watering. Occasional cutting back is necessary.

PROPAGATION BY DIVISION.

**4.** With most ground covers, a little goes a long way. A small division of camomile or dichondra planted 6" apart will in 1 season cover the space between. Once established, they require little care beyond watering and occasional cutting back or filling in.

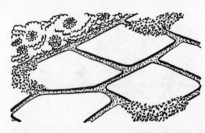

**5.** Another use for low ground-covering material is between stepping stones. Don't overplant or plant those which will become too large or floppy. Thymes, particularly the Woolly Thyme and the tiny-leaved *Thymus albus, Convolvulus mauritanicus* and some of the small dianthus are good for this.

**6.** The covering of banks and steep slopes presents many problems. A good way to handle them is to plant with a firm-rooted, solid-growing ground cover, such as ivy, vinca, creeping strawberry, helianthemums, or dwarf shrubs, such as cistus or cotoneaster.

# HERB GARDENS

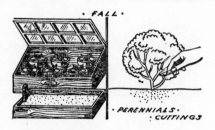

**1.** Herbs are among the easiest plants to grow. They ask little beyond sun and fairly light, well drained soil. Most of them can be propagated from seed sown either in flats or in the open ground. A few, such as tarragon, are grown from cuttings, while other perennial herbs are divided.

**4.** Old plaster and the mortar from between bricks are excellent for lightening and sweetening the soil in herb gardens. No manure or commercial fertilizers are necessary. The most fragrant and oil-filled herbs are those grown in rather poor, well drained, warm soil.

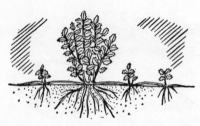

**2.** Very few herbs ask for more moisture than nature provides. Mints are an exception. They like partial shade and plenty of moisture at the roots. Propagate by division. The list of mints is long, and includes spearmint, peppermint, orange mint, apple mint and pennyroyal, or corn mint.

**5.** Many herbs, annual and perennial, can and should be sown in the ground. Later, when they have grown to 1" or 2", they can be thinned out. In all but mild climates, sow in spring when the ground is warm. Some can be lifted and carried over in frames.

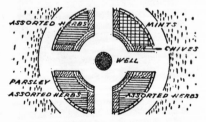

**3.** Herbs are best grown alone in small beds. A formal plan is good; or one can grow them in the vegetable garden, or narrow beds separated by paths. Some central feature holds the plan together. Edge beds with thyme, parsley, chives or basil. Let the outside hedges be of lavender or rosemary.

**6.** As a rule, herbs are not long lived. Lavenders, sage, thyme, and rosemary die out or become woody and unattractive after 5 to 7 years and must be replaced. A yearly cutting back is necessary for most herbs and is usually carried out in the fall.

# LAWNS

**1.** A beautiful lawn, except in most favored climates, requires exacting preparation and subsequent care. The first attention must be given to drainage. If it is naturally poor, the topsoil should be removed, saved for future use, and the subsoil broken up.

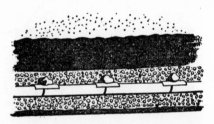

**2.** Breaking up of the hard subsoil may be sufficient in most cases. However, where a bad condition exists and a perfect lawn is desired, some such drainage system as that illustrated will be required and, in the long run, will be worth the time, effort and money expended.

**3.** After the drainage problem has been solved —during which time aeration of the subsoil has been also achieved—the topsoil can be replaced. If the soil is poor, haul in enough good rich loam to cover the lawn area to a depth of 6". At the same time, add fertilizer (weedless manure or turf food).

**4.** After preparing the top surface, water to bring up the weeds. In new locations, repeat this two, or better, three times, hoeing down weeds after they come up. Just before sowing, level and rake smoothly and finely. Then roll.

**5.** After rolling, sow the seed, fine or coarse, depending on the type of lawn required, the purpose for which it is used, and the district or climate. Scatter seed in two directions, lengthwise and crosswise. The amount of seed required varies with the type, but 1 pound to 150 square feet is a general or average amount.

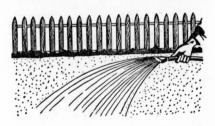

**6.** Some recommend raking in seed with fairly long, gentle strokes, while others prefer to chop it in with very light, even strokes of the rake. After raking, water with a fine spray. Keep damp until grass is up. When grass is 3" high, weed, and cut with blades set 2" high.

# ROCK GARDENS

**1.** The ideal rock garden is that which is placed naturally, with outcropping of rocks, on slopes or in small, though well drained swales, unless bog plants are used. Sun is preferable, though half shade is sometimes an advantage in California. A rock garden is best by itself.

**4.** A rock garden on a flat surface looks as if it "belonged." Use a plan. Excavate soil from what will be paths to 1' and throw this soil where needed. Use no boulders in small gardens. Proportion, balance, restraint and some variety are needed to make a good rock garden.

**2.** If good drainage is not present, excavate soil and fill with coarse gravel or clinkers and cover with a compost usually light and gritty in texture. Rocks should be few and not much in evidence. Lay them on their broadest sides and bury about ½ in the ground, sloping backward to carry water to the roots.

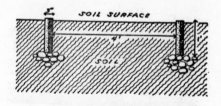

**5.** The diagram shows how to provide drainage where the soil is heavy and apt to prevent free movement of water. Underground watering by means of a perforated pipe, laid horizontally beneath the surface, is another aid to good rock gardens, especially those planted with alpines.

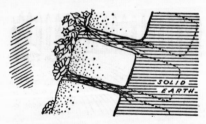

**3.** Work from the lowest to the highest section. Some prefer to plant as they place the rocks; others plant later on. Soil must be packed firmly about roots so that no drying air pockets will form. Avoid using very hard rocks, which hold no moisture.

**6.** Rock plants include true alpines, succulents, choice and dwarf shrubs, special rock plants and bog plants. Plant in bold masses, with few, rather than many varieties. Main plantings are best made in early spring. A March or April top dressing, following cutting back, is good.

# VEGETABLE GARDENS

**1.** Vegetables demand careful cultivation. Many plants stand drought and neglect; vegetables do not. Constant attention to watering, hoeing and harvesting is necessary. On the other hand, the advantage of having fresh, home-grown vegetables is worth the trouble it takes to grow them.

**4.** Cabbage, cauliflower and Brussels sprouts are winter and early-spring vegetables. Grow from seed started in autumn or early spring in a frame, greenhouse or hotbed. Prick out when large enough to handle and plant out when about 6″ high. They like a fairly heavy, rich soil, plenty of water and not too much heat.

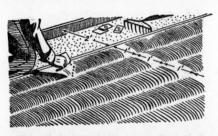

**2.** Root vegetables include carrots, beets, turnips, radishes and parsnips. All can be sown in autumn for early spring harvesting, or in spring for summer harvesting. Never manure the ground for these vegetables, for it will cause splitting of the roots. Soil manured for a previous crop will be rich enough.

CORN.
CABBAGE
CARROTS

**5.** A large measure of the success in growing vegetables is due to regular watering and cultivating. Weeds have no place in a well kept vegetable garden. Rotation of crops is desirable. For instance, let root crops follow leaf crops, such as spinach or cabbage.

**3.** Prepare soil many weeks ahead. Before planting, rake smoothly. Sow seed thickly in shallow drills; cover lightly. As they grow, thin out. Sow radishes every 2 weeks. Slow and fast crops (i. e., carrots and radishes or non-heading lettuce) can be sown together and the fast crop used first.

**6.** Vegetables grown in deep, moisture-holding soils, particularly in winter, need little watering. However, spring and summer vegetables require irrigation. Overhead sprinkling is simplest, but frequently beats down the soil and sometimes causes sunburn. Furrow irrigation is good, but slower.

# WATER GARDENS

**1.** A water garden is best used as a part of another design, such as a rose, iris or wild garden. Place where it will get sun, away from deciduous trees, with shelter from cold winds and in a low part of the garden, since water seeks the lowest level.

**4.** Most water plants, such as lilies, require 1' of soil, covered with 1' of water. They do best planted directly into the soil. In small water gardens, plant in boxes or tubs with space for 1 cubic foot of soil for each lily (or 1' square and deep). Fill with compost of 4 parts rich loam and 1 part rotted cow manure.

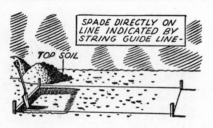

SPADE DIRECTLY ON LINE INDICATED BY STRING GUIDE LINE

TOP SOIL

**2.** The size of the pool should be in proportion to the garden. If a formal pool, construction must be exact, beginning with excavation. Stake it out so that no filling, which causes uneven settling, will be necessary. When removing topsoil, place it aside to use for some good purpose.

**5.** In frosty regions, all plants, including lilies, should be taken up and stored in wet sand. The water is then drained out, the pool filled with straw and the top covered with boards. There is a water garden for every special place. Well heads work charmingly into herb, vegetable and old-fashioned gardens.

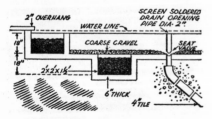

2" OVERHANG
WATER LINE
COARSE GRAVEL
SCREEN SOLDERED DRAIN OPENING PIPE DIA- 2"
SEAT VALVE
18"
18"
2"x2"x1½"
6" THICK
4" TILE

**3.** The depth of a formal pool should vary to allow for different types of planting; 3' is usually enough. Concrete and reinforced concrete are the usual materials. If not reinforced, no pool should be over 3' deep. Where there is danger of frost below the soil surface, fill in with rocks around the concrete foundation.

**6.** Bird baths can be formal, informal, sophisticated or rustic, but in any case, are best when simple. They belong in secluded spots where birds can really enjoy them. One can either fill them with a hose or have a trickle of water (but only a trickle!). Wall fountains are also appropriate for quiet spots.

# WINDOW BOXES

**1.** Window boxes are useful for town houses. They are not suitable for every type of house, and the material chosen, whether wood, metal, concrete or tile, must conform to that of the house. Drainage by means of ¾" holes or cracks along the bottom is necessary.

**4.** It is also possible to grow plants in pots which can be sunk in peat or soil in the box. Thus it is possible to keep rotating without lapses of bloom. Fuchsias, campanulas, begonias, lobelia, cinerarias, ivies, ferns and other foliage plants are adapted to shady window boxes.

**2.** Proper drainage is aided by tipping boxes backward slightly. Place a layer of rough material in the bottom, then the well mixed compost. Settle before planting. Soil in window boxes should be changed once a year. A reserve box can be kept on hand to replace that containing exhausted plants.

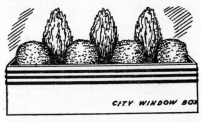

**5.** Stone, tile or metal boxes are best suited to city houses. City-dwellers can sink potted plants into the soil. It is best to change the soil once or twice a year, before it becomes sour. Evergreens and conifers, supplemented with trailing or upright foliage plants, or bulbs, are appropriate.

**3.** A great variety of plants can be grown in window boxes. Tender plants can quite easily be protected from frosts and awnings give summer shade. The planting is determined by the exposure. Petunias, geraniums, lantanas, nasturtiums, verbenas, and various bulbs are happy in sunny boxes.

**6.** Keep the soil well stirred and give at least one good soaking a week. Feed with liquid manure or balanced commercial fertilizer when plants are coming into bloom. A top dressing of well decayed manure or of topsoil mixed with bonemeal is good for permanently planted window boxes.

# INDEX